CRYSTAL ENERGY

FOR YOUR HOME

CRYSTAL ENERGY

FOR YOUR HOME

Creating Harmony in
Every Room

Ken and Joules Taylor

Sterling Publishing Co., Inc.
New York

Library of Congress Cataloging in Publication Data Available

1 2 3 4 5 6 7 8 9 10

First published in Great Britain in 2006 by Godsfield Press,
a division of Octopus Publishing Group Ltd
2–4 Heron Quays, London E14 4JP, England
Copyright © Octopus Publishing Group Ltd 2006
Text copyright © Ken and Joules Taylor 2006

Published in the U.S. in 2006 by Sterling Publishing Co., Inc.
387 Park Avenue South, New York, NY 10016
Distributed in Canada by Sterling Publishing
c/o Canadian Manda Group, 165 Dufferin Street,
Toronto, Ontario, Canada M6K 3H6

For information about custom editions, special sales, premium
and corporate purchases, please contact Sterling Special Sales
Department at 800-805-5489 or specialsales@sterlingpub.com.

Manufactured in China

Sterling ISBN 13: 978-1-4027-3331-4
          ISBN 10: 1-4027-3331-3

CONTENTS

INTRODUCTION

Enjoying beauty is a personal, almost intimate experience, and bringing nature's treasury of sparkling and colorful gems into your home can be a pure delight.

In the same way that the various rooms in your home suit different purposes (ranging from a romantic bedroom to a multipurpose living room), so the wide variety of natural crystals can match your full spectrum of moods. By using crystals to enhance certain emotions, through positioning them in different rooms around your home, you can energize those rooms to support the activities that you wish to promote.

Knowing which crystals affect which areas of your life is the key to creating a harmonious living space. Placing them to best advantage in the rooms of your home is like scattering seeds onto a fertile field, and their subtle, yet cumulative psychological influence works continuously to help you make your dreams come true.

Using techniques derived from the ancient Chinese art of placement, which is based on globally applicable observations of nature, you can explore the full scope of your life from the comfort of your own home. You can, for example, discover which crystals help stimulate a healthy sex life in the bedroom, and which can excite children's imagination to help them learn as they play in the nursery.

With an increasing number of people working from home, the home office has become an important area, which may be improved by crystals associated with generating wealth or good luck. Other crystals can help foster the spirit of nurturing that dwells in every kitchen, whose health-giving food nourishes family and friends, encourage and augment the bonds of friendship and love, or even act as a focus for study.

HOW TO USE THIS BOOK

Like people, crystals seem to have their own individual characters: some may inspire romance, love, or even spirituality; others may be protective or simply decorative to have on display. Inviting crystals into your home is as natural as having friends over to visit. However, just as you would think twice before allowing strangers into your life, so it makes sense to get to know your crystals properly. This book has been designed to help you match the most appropriate crystals to your rooms, moods, and activities.

We are all on a journey that, like the seasons of the year, leads inexorably from beginning to end, yet life is never predictable. In fact the world surrounds you with many unexpected opportunities—it is as if you are walking in a hall with many doors leading from it, and you can explore them more or less at random. This book accommodates both of these seemingly contradictory aspects of life: you can either opt to read it right through from start to finish, or simply dip in wherever you feel inclined. However, to make the best use of the information presented in the nine chapters, it is advisable to look through the remaining pages of this introduction.

A source of strength, safety, and tranquility, our home environment can be enhanced by the subtle use of nature's beautiful creations.

CRYSTAL **BASICS**

Although it is usual to speak in general terms about "crystals" in the home, about "healing crystals" or "protective crystals," this usually refers to a broad range of minerals, not all of which are actually crystals.

All crystals are minerals, but not all minerals are crystals. A crystal is formed when atoms or molecules join together in a natural design dictated by their atomic structure. A diamond, for example, forms a double pyramid shape that resembles the device on the playing-card suit of diamonds.

Not all minerals develop in this way, but many still enjoy positions of great prestige in crystal lore: opal, imperial jade, and pearl are non-crystalline minerals that can rival gemstones in value. Fortunately, there are many other crystals that are inexpensive, yet still possess valuable properties.

CHOOSING CRYSTALS

Whenever possible, you should visit a store that specializes in selling crystals, rather than shopping online, so that you can choose between a range of specimens. Never rush your decision; compare all the items on offer, and be prepared to come back another time or even to shop elsewhere, if you are not given time to browse at leisure. Ask for advice about keeping your chosen crystal clean.

Try to avoid chipped or damaged crystals, unless better ones are unavailable or unaffordable. Color is particularly important for talismans, or good-luck symbols, where a deep shade often works best. For stones intended to brighten a dark spot in the home, clarity is vital.

Crystals with natural patterns (such as the swirls and rings in malachite, the ferny shapes in moss agate, and the lacy effect in blue lace agate) can be the most challenging ones to select: sometimes a single large pattern works best; at other times an extreme range of patterns is preferable. Always look out for "apparitions"— patterns that appear to resemble something else (faces are most common)—which make interesting collections in their own right. One thing is certain: the biggest crystal isn't always the best. Size is very much

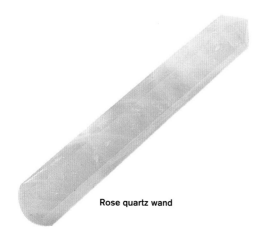

Rose quartz wand

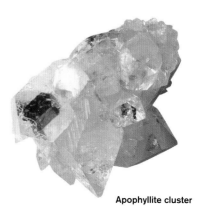

Apophyllite cluster

Bathing under running water—invigorating, enlivening, and refreshing—is the natural and effective method of cleansing most crystals.

CARE AND CLEANSING

Most crystals suitable for use in the home are robust, strong, and incredibly ancient. They should be treated with great respect, like old, wise, and treasured friends, but there's no need to handle them with excessive reverence. You can simply wipe the dust off most smooth crystals with a soft cloth, and rinse them with warm water (as a general rule, use as few chemicals as possible). Smooth crystals in particular may become slippery when wet, so always take care not to drop them when handling them.

Many people recommend magically cleansing crystals by immersing them in salt water. This practice inevitably leaves a residue of salt on the crystal, which will itself need to be cleaned away. It is preferable to follow a more natural tradition, such as allowing sunlight to bathe every part of the crystal. There is also a charming tradition that recommends cleansing crystals by leaving them to be bathed in moonlight during the night to enhance their qualities: to do this, simply place your crystals safely on a windowsill at full moon.

a matter of personal choice, although your crystal should be large enough that you can see it clearly and be able to handle it without it slipping through your fingers (unless it's a gemstone, in which case even tiny chips can be used talismanically).

Sourcing your specimens from an ethical supplier may greatly benefit the long-term enjoyment of your crystals, but you should always feel comfortable with your choice and positively cherish the chosen one. Sometimes an almost insignificant feature (or even a flaw) can make a particular crystal gel with you; it may take years to realize why this is so, but it can offer vital revelations about yourself.

Raw blue lace agate

Tumbled moss agate

THE CHINESE ART OF **PLACEMENT**

Nature has her own way of doing things and, unless you want trouble in your life, you'd better pay them due respect. Anyone who puts cacti on a shady windowsill will never see them thrive; and ferns placed in the full heat of the sun will perish, despite being given every other care and attention.

If you get the fundamentals right, then you're off to a great start—get them wrong and you're doomed to fail. Feng shui, or the ancient Chinese art of placement, is the art of living in harmony with your environment; it is only one of many essentially similar methods that developed in numerous cultures, but it was refined into an extraordinarily sophisticated practice that few other systems can rival.

The words "feng shui" mean wind and water respectively. They are the two elements that flow, and fluidity is the vital attribute of chi (known in Japan as ki and in the modern, pinyin transliteration as ji)—the Chinese word for boundless mystical energy that vivifies the universe. When chi can move freely, it is fertile and creative; when chi is blocked, it becomes stagnant, unwholesome, and even poisonous. Much of the work of the enthusiast of the Chinese art of placement involves simply ensuring that chi can flow through the home like a warm spring breeze. This brings a welcome freshness into every room and creates an atmosphere of energized peace that permeates every nook and cranny.

THE ROLE OF CRYSTALS IN PROMOTING BALANCE

Crystals are natural allies in the promotion of balance, bringing charm and beauty as well as a sense of stability, composure, and strength to the home. They can make a practical difference to any room: for instance, light-colored or reflective crystals instantly brighten dark places, whereas dark crystals fill plain areas with interest.

Tumbled black onyx

Tumbled jet

Polished obsidian

The simple elegance of the yin/yang symbol reveals the beauty of nature's effortless equilibrium. The contrast of dark and light reminds us that the one cannot be recognized without the other.

The Chinese art of placement makes a positive contribution to resolving conflicts and bringing opposing viewpoints into alignment. By learning how to apply its techniques to your home, you can not only improve your living space, but may even discover a radical new perspective, with the power to transform your entire life.

Above all, the Chinese art of placement is practical: simple actions such as moving cacti into the light and ferns into the shade will produce definite and predictable results. Learning the subtleties of the art of placement takes time and patience, but small, easily made improvements are cumulative in effect. Although each little alteration may seem trivial in itself, the only way to accomplish a great journey is one step at a time.

In the Chinese art of placement, as with so much else in life, as long as you are moving closer to your heart's desire, you cannot go far wrong.

The interplay of light and dark is a central theme in the Chinese art of placement: the terms "yang" and "yin" traditionally denoted the bright and shady sides of a hill respectively, although they now have a wider range of applications. Oriental philosophy regards harmony between light and dark as beneficial, and imbalance as evil and unhealthy. Change is natural and right: night is not to be feared when you understand that it is simply the transitory counterpart to day.

Tumbled seer stone

Quartz polished egg

Selenite pillar

THE FIVE **ELEMENTS**

Everyone responds emotionally to colors and patterns, and your personal tastes are instinctively reflected in your clothes and the way you choose to decorate your home. Crystals, too, readily generate this psychological impact: jewelry comprising blood-red gems reveals wild passions, whereas pale-blue crystals indicate calm self-control. Because they can stimulate certain feelings, attitudes, and thoughts, crystals make very effective talismans.

Understanding the effects of crystals is more of an art than a science, and your personal intuition is probably your most valuable guide, although countless generations of natural philosophers have contributed to a treasury of insights.

The Chinese tradition classified all of nature into five categories, which can be imagined as the four arms of a cross, plus its center. The four arms indicate the cardinal points of the compass (north, south, east, and west; also associated with the pole, the equator, sunrise, and sunset respectively), and this simple idea may be used to harmonize your home with its landscape and to align yourself with your environment. Each of these areas is associated with a particular element: wood with sunrise, fire with the equator, metal with sunset, water with the pole, and earth with the center. A surfeit or lack of one element over another will result in a lack of balance and harmony, and should therefore be avoided wherever possible—or eased by adding crystals representing the lacking element.

Raw emerald

WOOD

Associated with the rising sun and springtime, this element symbolizes the urge of life to grow and thrive. Its energy can be imagined as flowing upward like a seedling that becomes a tree. Its color is green, and minerals such as green jade and crystals like emerald are strongly represented. Its archetypal shape is the column, and a massage wand (a crystal wand used to massage the skin, see page 21) is a perfect likeness, although a natural tourmaline crystal also embodies this elemental shape. Traditionally, wood is represented by the green dragon.

FIRE

The heat of the sun at noon, of high summer, and of the equator suggests the exuberance and activity of this element. Sharp tongues of red flame rising into the air evoke its key

Faceted ruby

shape, the point. The naturally angular facets of quartz are excellent examples; the pyramidal point of the apophyllite crystal is an ideal fiery shape; translucent red crystals, such as faceted ruby, are also perfect. Fire is represented by the red bird.

METAL

Tumbled specular hematite

Dusk and sunset are associated with the accomplishments of a fulfilled life—like ripe and nourishing autumn fruits. Metal, which is wrought through the skill and experience of craftspeople, represents maturity, knowledge, and restraint. Its traditional shape is domed, like the "bubbles" of malachite (itself an ore of copper), and its colors can be silvery, white (like milky quartz), or gray (like specular hematite). Its texture is smooth. Metal is represented by the white tiger.

EARTH

Earth represents the solid center: the core and the heart. Its shape is traditionally square, but any rectangle (or even a flat surface) is appropriate. The cube of an iron-pyrite crystal is the perfect expression of this shape, particularly as the color of earth is yellow. This element is usually considered opaque and rough, or granular in texture, like drusy quartz. There is no traditional animal to represent earth.

Cubic iron pyrite

WATER

Tumbled blue lace agate

This element sinks to the lowest place, and represents the sun at its invisible polar nadir and the cold dark of winter. The meandering stream is its natural shape, and its colors are blue and black. The swirling patterns of lace agate resemble eddying water, while deep-blue tiger's eye reveals the shifting illusions and dreamscape of night. Transparent stones are emblematic, as are smoothed or tumble-polished specimens. Water is represented by the black turtle.

THE NINE **ROOMS**

The Chinese art of placement originated in prehistoric farming communities that were made up of single-room dwellings in which the hearth was the family's focal point, and the single entrance/exit was a key psychological feature. During that time, and similarly today, a farmer's crops often grew best in fields that faced the south and many such pragmatic observations became the building blocks of the Chinese art of placement, enshrining a sensible way of living in harmony with nature.

It may seem surprising perhaps, that there is a good correlation between modern homes in the West and the *lo shu* grid of numbers that inspired the plan of nine chambers or rooms used in the Chinese art of placement.

USING CRYSTALS TO ENHANCE THE *LO SHU*

Each of the nine chapters in this book has a room devoted to it. Each chapter explores how crystals can enhance a room and also reveals practical ways in which crystals can help you make the most of life's opportunities as epitomized by that room.

The *lo shu* is treated as a map of the home, but houses can vary greatly from the "ideal" layout in the *lo shu.* Crystals provide an excellent approach to reconciling contemporary homes with the ancient, harmonious pattern. For example, the following chapters describe how crystals can compensate for problem areas in houses—dark corners or awkward seating arrangements—but also describes practical ways in which crystals can help you make the most of life's opportunities, as epitomized by that room.

Lo shu *in the northern hemisphere*

	SOUTH	
Wealth 4 Office	**Status** 9 Living room	**Relationships** 2 Bedroom
Family 3 Kitchen	**Center** 5 Sanctuary	**Children** 7 Children's rooms
Knowledge 8 Study	**Career** 1 Bathroom	**Helpful people** 6 Hallway

EAST (left) / WEST (right) / NORTH (bottom)

Lo shu *in the southern hemisphere*

	NORTH	
Relationships 2 Bedroom	**Status** 9 Living room	**Wealth** 4 Office
Children 7 Children's rooms	**Center** 5 Sanctuary	**Family** 3 Kitchen
Helpful people 6 Hallway	**Career** 1 Bathroom	**Knowledge** 8 Study

WEST (left) / EAST (right) / SOUTH (bottom)

Tumbled blue tiger's eye

Polished turquoise

Raw aventurine

Tumbled bloodstone

Here is a simple and inexpensive way of harmonizing your whole home.

♦ First, discover where the cardinal points are in your home; you can find this most easily with a compass.

♦ Then refer to the two lo shu grids on the facing page and find the one that applies to the hemisphere that you live in.

♦ Select one crystal from the list opposite and position it in your home, close to its corresponding compass point (indicated by the lo shu grid). You can put it out of the way in a drawer, display it prominently, or even bury it in the garden—it's up to you.

♦ Once the crystal is in position, it acts as an anchor, aligning your home to all the natural forces in the world. It can also help attune you to the cycles that shape your life.

♦ You can add more crystals at their appropriate positions, if you wish: many people build up a cross shape, using the four cardinal points.

Status
carnelian, red tiger's eye, garnet

Relationships
rhodochrosite, rhodonite, rose quartz

Children
milky quartz, optical calcite, specular hematite

Helpful people
quartz cluster, quartz wand, tourmalinated quartz

Career
black onyx, blue tiger's eye, lapis lazuli

Knowledge
chrysocolla, malachite with azurite, turquoise

Family
aventurine, chrysoprase, malachite

Wealth
bloodstone, red and green serpentine, unakite

Tumbled red tiger's eye

Tumbled rose quartz

Tumbled specular hematite

Tumbled tourmalinated quartz

1 BATHROOM
The framework of your life

This room is associated with the element of water and with the colors blue and black. The bathroom is also connected with the structures that underpin your life. In this chapter you will discover ways to combine crystals with cleansing routines, such as baths and showers, to help stimulate the body's chi energy and connect you with your dreams, goals, hopes and fears.

CRYSTALS FOR THE BATHROOM:
RELAXATION AND TRANQUILITY

Even the smallest bathroom can benefit from the addition of crystals—perhaps even more so than a large room. Of course, a capacious bathroom probably already has plenty of ornaments scattered about, and positioning a few new crystals among the scented candles will be simplicity itself.

Sadly, though, most bathrooms scarcely have enough space for the bare necessities. To overcome a lack of shelving space on which to display your crystals, you can hang them from the ceiling in the corners of the room, adding interest and sparkle to gloomy areas, but don't suspend crystal cascades (crystals threaded onto a cord) above your head where you lie in the bath, or directly above a toilet, for safety reasons.

The toilet is one of the least attractive features in the whole home, and is not a welcoming sight when it is immediately visible upon entering the bathroom. Erecting a bead screen is a good solution, particularly if it includes some beads of a black or dark-blue crystal, such as black onyx and lapis lazuli.

So that your eyes are not always drawn inexorably to the toilet, you can create a pleasant distraction in the form of a dangling crystal cascade or even a solitary hanging crystal (a rock-quartz wand with natural facets is ideal). Hanging this between the door and the toilet is traditional, but may be impractical if you have a low ceiling. An effective alternative is to hang the crystals from a hook on an adjacent wall.

SOOTHING BATHROOM CRYSTALS

In general, specialized crystals for the bathroom should be blue or black and as large as is practical. Whenever possible, choose crystals that will be useful as well as decorative, such as massage wands. These crystal wands are polished to a high standard and are used to massage the skin and underlying muscles; they are

Tumbled sodalite

Tumbled blue lace agate

Tumbled lapis lazuli

Tumbled smoky quartz

usually about 5 inches long and 1 inch wide, and the best ones are narrower at one end than the other. Massage wands may be used with proprietary massage oils and suitable aromatherapy oils, but remember that polished stones can be slippery when wet. A wide variety of smooth, hand-size crystals can also be used as massage stones. Here are some suggestions to remedy particular situations.

- Polished lace agate aids relaxation and, especially during a long soak in the bath, can prompt your subconscious to answer questions that may be troubling you. The bathroom is where you daily face the naked truth about yourself, and is the ideal place to consider who you are and what you'd like to be.
- A celestite cluster placed in a bright spot brings the warmth and tranquility of the summer sky down to Earth, and is helpful in calming emotional turmoil.
- The shiny elegance of polished smoky quartz can fit into any decorating scheme, while sodalite is a deep blue crystal that adds instant character to a nondescript decor.
- Lapis lazuli is a popular and attractive bathroom crystal, and is often carved into ornaments that bring a personal touch to this room. Its golden flecks set in a deep dusky-blue stimulate appreciation of the little personal pleasures that can help to make long or tedious hours more bearable.
- Any blue or black crystal carved into a turtle (ideally) or tortoise shape, and prominently displayed on a windowsill or bright shelf, acts as a reminder that to enjoy life you need to make time to care for yourself. Flying off in the wrong direction is far worse than making slow but steady progress in the right direction.

It is essential, in your busy life, to take a little time to pamper yourself, indulge your senses, treat yourself to some "me" time...

STIMULATE **CHI CIRCULATION**

Chi—life energy—sustains and animates all things, including those normally classified as inanimate, such as crystals. To operate properly, chi needs to flow. Stagnant air or water soon becomes poisonous, and a buildup of pressure (behind a dam or in a vein, for example) can be deadly. Although stagnant chi doesn't have quite such dangerous physical consequences, its more subtle effects can pollute both mind and spirit.

Chi circulates through the body as well as through the home, keeping you healthy and vigorous. However, the stresses of modern life can lead to obstructions in the flow of chi, and this is often blamed for persistent irritability, headaches, and aches and pains that have no other cause. After a busy day spent in an office or dealing with the problems of others, you need—and deserve—time to yourself, to repair the damage.

The bathroom should be your first port of call, if at all possible. Take time to bathe: a shower to cleanse yourself, followed by a bath to relax in, is ideal. While you gently remove the outward grime of the day with a sponge, brush, or body buffer, imagine the stress sliding from you and washing away with the water. Try using a pumice stone (an abrasive natural rock formed from volcanic cinders) to remove any hard skin. Once you feel clean, turn your attention to your inner self.

Turn your bathroom into a tranquil haven where you release the stresses of the busy day.

CRYSTAL MASSAGE

Every bathroom should have at least one massage wand or some large egg-shaped massage stones. These are not only beautifully decorative, but also extremely useful. Choose blue or black stones: sodalite is an excellent and readily available mineral, traditionally useful for banishing the fear of things beyond your control and for calming the mind; black onyx can help you to confront and overcome negative emotions; blue lace agate is a deeply cleansing crystal, and stimulates the subconscious to prepare the way for personal development and growth.

- ♦ Stroke your chosen crystal over your body slowly and gently—the aim is to encourage the flow of chi, not to bruise yourself.

- ♦ Start at your heart and stroke outward, moving down your legs and arms and upward to your head. Then reverse the motion, stroking gently back toward your heart.

- ♦ Visualize bright energy following the movement of the crystal—your chi flowing smoothly through your body.

- ♦ Become aware of the tides within you, your blood circulating, your lungs filling and emptying—feel these individual elements of your body working together to sustain life.

- ♦ Focus your mind on the sensation of the crystal, its texture and hardness, while your eyes relax and enjoy its color against your skin. A sensation of warmth under the crystal as it moves is perfectly natural, as is a feeling of tranquility after the massage.

- ♦ Once you've finished, try to take things calmly and move slowly for the next hour or so, in order to receive the full benefit of this exercise.

Angelite massage wand

FLOAT **FREE**

With your body cleansed, and chi flowing freely through your physical form, it's time to turn your attention inward a little. By relaxing your mind and body, you can let your spirit soar and reveal a glimpse of the whole person you are—a unique mixture of characteristics. Then you can begin to see how you may grow and evolve to become the person you feel you could (and perhaps should) be.

Turn your bathroom into a personal sanctuary: lock the door and shut out the outside world. Run a bath and add some bath crystals (preferably blue) with the tiniest pinch of salt (the most readily available cleansing crystal). Few people have a bath large enough to serve as an improvised sensory deprivation tank, where you can float freely without external influences intruding, but it's sufficient that the water can take some of your weight, and those soluble crystals will add a touch of extra buoyancy.

Serene, calm, and tranquil—let your bathroom become your refuge from the cares of the world. Here you can learn to listen to your heart.

To set the scene, light some candles, scented if possible—lavender is an excellent relaxing and cleansing fragrance—and place one candle where its light can illuminate a crystal held in your hands. Position another crystal where you can see it easily from a lying position: at the end of the bath, on a shelf or windowsill. Although not essential for this exercise, its beauty will always remind you of your aspiration to integrate nature's gifts into your life. Now you can begin.

♦ Immerse yourself in the warmly welcoming water. Feel comfortable in it, and try to make yourself aware of the sensation of floating, however slightly.

♦ Hold a crystal in your hand. An egg- or gourd-shaped one is ideal; a blue "goldstone," which seems to be full of stars, or a smoky quartz for realism and pragmatism, is also perfect for this exercise.

♦ Place your chosen crystal on your chest, resting it on your skin, and hold it gently in place. Breathe slowly and deeply, consciously relaxing. Imagine yourself as your own Pole Star, with the rest of the universe revolving around you.

♦ You feel centered, completely in control of all that affects you, and at peace with yourself. You are distanced from the stresses of your daily life. You can find new insights, see new perspectives, and envisage a new you.

♦ Consider who you are now, then consider who you want to be. Ignore the impossible. While it's nice to dream about fame, beauty, and wealth, you should think about the fundamentals: the inner aspects of yourself that you love and hate. Even that jealous streak, that habitual miserliness, or tendency to gossip about others is part of the person you are, and that person deserves the opportunity to grow.

♦ If "home is where the heart is," then your own body is your home, and the still center of it (like the Pole Star) is your heart. Focus on your positive aspects. Think of the good things you've done, the people you've made happy, the satisfaction to be gained from simple acts of thoughtfulness. Consciously decide to do more. Making that decision is the first step toward creating the reality.

♦ Give yourself time to settle, letting the new you really sink in and feel at home in your body, before getting out of the bath. Then spend a few minutes looking at yourself in the mirror. Try not to see the outer body, but the inner self shining like the star it really is.

Tumbled smoky quartz

LEARN TO **LOVE YOURSELF**

As well as being a place for cleansing and centering yourself, the bathroom can be a space where you start putting your dreams into practice. Check that it offers a relaxing environment, free of unnecessary clutter, and try to make it a pleasant and comfortable place to be. You may already have introduced some blue or black crystals into your bathroom and gained some experience with crystal massage to soothe your body (see pages 20–21), and you should have practiced calming and centering yourself (see pages 22–23).

In such a place you can now observe the structure of your mind and consider how chi can energize your life. You can also explore ways to overcome the things that are holding you back from being who you want to be.

Everyone suffers from negative emotions, inhibitions, and mental blocks from time to time. Some of these are useful—a good cry helps release the stress that comes with grief, and a fear of being punished can prevent harm of other people—but they may also restrict your growth and cause great unhappiness.

A CRYSTAL CONTEMPLATION

Iolite, which is also known as water sapphire, is a beautiful dichromatic (two-colored) crystal. Viewed along one axis, its color is a delicate, almost-transparent blue-green; viewed along another axis, it is a deep, translucent violet-blue. This internal ambiguity celebrates difference and encourages tolerance, both toward yourself and for others. A small, natural piece of iolite makes the perfect crystal to assist you in learning to love yourself for what you are—even with your unresolved contradictions.

Use it as a contemplation crystal while you're soaking in the bath, holding and handling it so that you can see how its appearance changes as you turn it in the light. However, it is not the crystal that changes—just your perception of it.

Reflect on your moods: iolite teaches that your perception of yourself alters depending on how you feel, and yet all your images of yourself are valid and of real worth. Let this knowledge inspire your self-confidence. Keep the crystal in the bathroom, near the mirror, where you can see it every time you enter the room, as a constant reminder of how unique and precious you are.

Raw iolite

ASSESS YOURSELF

A lack of self-confidence or self-respect represents a major obstacle to pursuing your dreams and finding your path through life, so it helps to scrutinize yourself carefully and evaluate what you see.

♦ Stand in the bathroom and take a good look at yourself in the mirror. All too often you probably allow yourself to be manipulated into believing that you should measure up to someone else's ideals. But here, in your own home, it's safe and wise to be honest with yourself.

♦ Do you like what you see? Most people will like some aspects of themselves, but not all.

♦ You could of course make some external changes to bring your body more into line with your mental image of yourself: jewelry can be helpful in obscuring or accentuating certain aspects of your appearance, drawing attention away from a feature you don't like and toward one you do.

♦ However, this will accomplish little unless your mind, body, and spirit are fully involved in the process. So read on to discover ways to achieve this.

AMBITIONS, HOPES, AND FEARS

Every new day is rich with opportunities and with challenges to keep you alert, treading a fine line between your personal hopes and fears.

Acting spontaneously can generate an interesting and exciting life that brings great rewards. However, too much chaos can cause major problems, such as being unprepared for important events or treating people in a flippant, offhand way. At worst you can start to feel like a ship in a storm, and may even sense that your life is trickling away down the drain. At such times it is sensible to steady your mind by fixing your sights on a long-term goal or an inspiring idea toward which you can focus and steer—a kind of guiding star.

Finding a crystal to represent that "star" can take a little effort, but this book will provide plenty of suggestions. For now, you can simply set up a target, which should embody one of your current wishes: to make better use of crystals in the home.

An obsidian sphere is ideal for this purpose, but other black or blue crystals mentioned in this chapter will also work. The crystal that you select is going to become a psychological magnet, pulling your thoughts toward your chosen goal. It will work like a mentor, energizing you to pursue that goal, and will be a tangible link with your future achievements—your crystal will act as a talisman.

Velvet obsidian sphere

ENERGIZE A TALISMAN

Making a talisman is rather like charging a battery, except that instead of using electricity, you concentrate your thoughts and emotions into the crystal.

♦ Lie in a warm bath: this is an ideal place to gather your thoughts and start working up your enthusiasm.

♦ Close your eyes and place the crystal on your chest over your heart, or hold it to your forehead, all the time visualizing the energy of your aspiration soaking in among the atoms of the crystal and permeating its structure.

♦ You can recharge your talisman repeatedly, and at any time, simply by focusing your desire into the crystal itself. You don't even need to touch it: simply thinking of it can do the trick. The same is true of using it: handling your talisman is the most direct way to draw on its strength, but simply knowing that it exists is enough.

♦ Have as many talismans as you like, but, at least to begin with, use them one at a time (store the others in a special small box or pouch—the crystals that work best will become personal treasures that you will want to keep for ever and revisit time and again).

♦ In the evening, when you glance in the bathroom mirror before climbing into bed, spare a thought for the day: its ups and downs, and how you fared.

♦ Let your talisman remind you of your goal and, even if its realization seems further away than ever, take comfort that your efforts have prepared you to meet tomorrow's opportunities and challenges more successfully.

PATTERNS OF **CHANGE AND BALANCE**

It may seem obvious, but every function in the bathroom involves water: cleansing, cleaning, flushing away waste, removing what is not wanted, what has served its purpose, so that your health may be maintained and growth made possible.

The bathroom is the one room that everyone uses daily, which makes it the ideal place to begin introducing crystals into your home. Placing crystals where they can be seen and handled frequently is sensible if you wish to obtain maximum benefit from them.

TALISMANIC CRYSTALS FOR CHANGE

Some things cannot be changed: you might say they are fated to be, and should be accepted with good grace. Other aspects of life can be enlivened, made healthier and more fulfilling; this is especially true of the elements that make up your own personality and lifestyle.

You can use the following crystals as meditation stones (see pages 22–23, substituting the crystals given below) while lying in the bath. Some of them make lovely jewelry as well.

- Angelite represents aspiration and the willingness to give up old ideas in order to allow new comprehension to take hold.
- Apatite calms and alleviates nervous tension.
- Azurite helps to overcome the fear of making mistakes, and teaches you to learn from them.
- Nacreous ammonite is a beautiful marine fossil that symbolizes the wisdom and compassion that come with age after a life well spent.
- Turquoise encourages contemplation, and helps you to resist temptation. Its beautiful summer-blue color is also excellent for relieving stress. If you are wearing it as jewelry, be sure to wear three separate pieces.

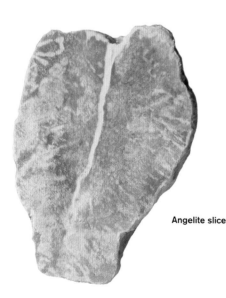

Angelite slice

Blue apatite polished egg

Raw azurite

CRYSTALS FOR COSMIC BALANCE

Most of life involves a threefold process. In broad terms, the systems of the body work in cycles of threes: inhalation, the absorption of oxygen, exhalation; eating, digestion, excretion; birth, life, death. Recognizing that such patterns are inevitable helps you to adapt to change, freeing you to focus on what is really important. And, by flushing away what is finished with, you are better able to make the best use of your life.

Many cultures, both ancient and modern, perceive a threefold division to the universe. In the Chinese art of placement this materializes as Heaven above (yang), the Earth below (yin), and Humanity in the middle, acting as the balance between the other two. Maintaining the balance between yin and yang is essential for the health of mind, body, and spirit.

The following crystals, used as meditation stones in the bathroom, act as a reminder that two different characteristics can not only coexist, but can together produce a unique and beautiful whole.

- Blue tiger's eye strengthens resolve and helps to overcome manipulative tendencies (both your own and those of others toward you). It is also called falcon's eye.
- Lapis lazuli promotes harmony and the ability to take charge of your own life.
- Larvikite is protective and promotes sophisticated thought processes. It also helps to integrate the multiple facets of your personality.
- Spectrolite assists in uncovering hidden abilities so that they may be used to further your dreams, especially those relating to your career.

Tumbled blue tiger's eye

Polished turquoise

Tumbled lapis lazuli

Raw labradorite

2 BEDROOM
Friendship and love

This room is associated with the element of earth and with the colors yellow and pink. It is concerned with friends and lovers, with the pleasures and pains of social connections, and with falling in love. In this chapter you will learn to use crystals to aid restful sleep, enhance courtship and romance, sex and stamina, partnerships and supportive friendships.

CRYSTALS FOR THE BEDROOM:
DREAMS OF PASSION

If all you want is a good night's sleep, then your bedroom can become your personal sanctuary (see pages 72–85). However, if you don't want to sleep alone, your bedroom needs to accommodate a different set of qualities.

To attract a long-term mate, it's important to ensure that your bedroom, in particular, is decorated in a fashion that would enable a partner to feel at home. If your bedroom reflects purely yin characteristics of femininity, softness, darkness, and silence, then yang won't be comfortable and will probably be scared away. Likewise, a room full of loud music, bright lights, strong colors, and angular or sharp objects will significantly reduce the chances of attracting someone who is looking for a little tenderness and romance.

HARMONIOUS BEDROOM CRYSTALS

Even if you can't do much about your bedroom's decor, you can use crystals to help correct an imbalance of yin or yang. Light-colored or transparent crystals add an element of yang, particularly if they are slightly angular (a quartz wand is a prime example), whereas dark or curvaceous crystals embody yin characteristics.

- A sphere is ideal in the bedroom, because this shape is a powerful symbol of unity and completion. A similar effect can be achieved with approximately circular slices of agate and with round, polished crystals.
- Rhodochrosite is a beautiful pink crystal that is often used as a talisman to overcome feelings of shyness and nervousness, help the body relax, and increase strength.

Rose quartz heart

Tumbled rhodochrosite

Tumbled rhodonite

- Rhodonite, in beautiful shades of pink, is another perfect crystal for the bedroom, as it helps foster a sense of proportion and humor—important elements for increasing the stability of a relationship.
- A rose-quartz crystal carved in a heart shape is an excellent combination of curvy pastel yin and translucent yang elements. Hang it from your bedside lamp or above the headboard of your bed to invite love into your room. Or, if your bed is against a wall, put it on that wall instead to help dispel any feelings of confinement or loss of freedom of expression that could oppress whoever sleeps against the wall. Rose quartz enjoys an association with love and nurturing, and has a calming, soothing influence, ideal for establishing a harmonious atmosphere in the bedroom – regardless of the fireworks that may ensue later.

A key position in which to place these crystals is the first

Even the smallest bedroom can become a place of powerful, positive emotions; a place to recharge ourselves ready to face the outside world.

place you notice when you enter the bedroom. Another perfect spot is directly in front of you when you sit up in bed. If your bedroom door is situated there, hang a single crystal ball from the ceiling midway between you and the door: this will help prevent the positive chi generated in the bedroom from leaking out.

Rooms with a view facing the sunrise or sunset are traditionally deemed to make the best bedrooms and, unless you have children (see pages 104–105), you can please yourself as to which direction you choose. However, if you are looking to turn your bedroom into a love nest, plenty of early morning sunshine would help wake you up after those late nights of passion.

SET **THE SCENE**

The intimacy of the bedroom is different from that of the bathroom: while the latter is, in the main, a place to be private by yourself, the bedroom is very often somewhere to be intimate with others.

To make a new start in this important room you should clear any clutter—particularly anything that evokes painful memories of a failed relationship. If you can't bear to part with certain items, such as gifts of jewelry, at least tidy them away into another room (the study, or your place of sanctuary perhaps). Ensure there is space in your bedroom for someone else to keep their clothes and other personal items.

INSPIRING CRYSTALS

Once your bedroom is prepared, use crystals to promote the free flow of chi and good fortune.

- A pink or golden-colored crystal carved in the shape of a bird (any kind of bird, but a pair of mandarin ducks in particular is a symbol of romance and fidelity) and placed facing toward the equator is ideal.
- Rose quartz promotes love.
- Amethyst symbolizes intuition.
- Tiger's eye fosters an understanding of your personal inner resources.
- Citrine aids communication and clarity of thought.
- Smooth textures and rounded shapes are most suitable, while a variety of color shades and opacities symbolizes the range of people who share your life— and the choices you may make as to which of them become friends and which lovers.

Raw citrine

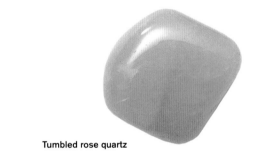

Tumbled rose quartz

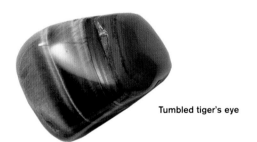

Tumbled tiger's eye

Tumbled amethyst

CLEANSE THE BEDROOM

To exorcize really old, stale chi, get a pair of piezoelectric quartz crystals. These remarkable "glow stones" are natural forms of the oscillator that is used at the heart of quartz watches and clocks; they are often available from stores that stock scientific curiosities for children. Their molecules are arranged in such a way that when the crystal's atomic lattice is deformed by pressure (the knocking together that you will perform), its negatively charged silicon atoms are pushed slightly to one side, while its positively charged oxygen atoms are squeezed to the other side. This electrical imbalance produces a current within the crystal, making it glow, as harmless (but distinct) electric sparks flare within it.

♦ Knock the piezoelectric crystals together nine times.

♦ As the cleansing of your bedroom should take place during daylight, the actual flashes won't be visible, so you should familiarize yourself with this unusual natural phenomenon in a darkened room, before using the quartz crystals to clear away stagnant chi. Experiment by scratching one crystal on the other, or by scraping them together, as well as simply knocking them.

♦ After the violence of the nine flashes, rub the crystals together with a circular motion, to produce a long-lasting afterglow that penetrates every nook and cranny of the bedroom, dispersing the stagnant chi.

ENCOURAGE **DREAMING**

Sleep: everyone needs it to rest and recharge the body. Likewise everyone needs to dream, even if you can't actually remember your dreams. Dreaming is the mind's way of resting, of sorting through the events and experiences of the last spell of wakefulness, and of preparing itself for the future—allowing the chi of the mind to flow. If people aren't allowed to dream, they may become psychotic.

It's therefore important that the place in which you sleep is conducive to dreaming. Its chi should flow smoothly, your bedroom's colors and contours should be soft and soothing, and the bed must be comfortable. However, the bedroom often serves more purposes than the mere function of sleeping, and finding a compromise between these different uses can be tricky. A room designed for passion may not be the most restful place in which to sleep (and vice versa), but there are steps you can take to make the best of your bedroom.

Soft pastel colors for the walls, with deep warm colors on the floor and at the windows, can make a fantastic backdrop for vibrantly colored furnishings and bedclothes. And taking inspiration from crystals is an excellent way to start.

- Sugilite is ideal for this purpose. Its bands of color range from hot pink to deep purple, and the crystal itself helps to smooth transitions, as well as acting to keep the peace and encourage a mellow atmosphere.
- Charoite, a softer crystal with swirling shades of purple, helps creative thinking and mental resourcefulness.
- Keeping both these crystals beside your bed will act as a balance for the room's various functions.
- A piece of polished, pale rose quartz rubbed gently over your forehead before switching off the light will aid restful sleep. This crystal promotes love of all kinds, including self-love and forgiveness.

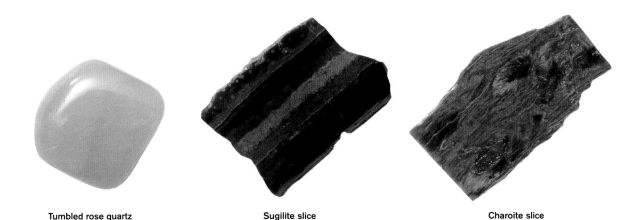

Tumbled rose quartz   Sugilite slice   Charoite slice

KEEP A DREAM DIARY

Your dreams give you an insight into the way your mind works. They can often indicate problems before they reach your conscious mind, or can present you with solutions to concerns that have been troubling you during your waking hours. You would be wise to listen to what your subconscious is trying to teach you, and an ideal way to do this is to keep a dream diary.

♦ Use a journal or notebook kept solely for this purpose, and place a large piece of pale amethyst on top (amethyst enhances intuition and artistic abilities).

♦ Get into the habit of thinking through your dreams before you rise from bed and taking a few minutes to write them down.

♦ Don't be discouraged if you find this difficult at first. If there is a day or two when you simply don't have time, or can't remember your dreams at all, don't worry. More importantly, don't give up.

♦ Don't be tempted to use an A–Z dream dictionary to analyze your dreams. They are specific to you, and while it may take a little while for you to work out their meanings, it's worth it for the profound insights you will gain.

SEX CRYSTALS

There is no human activity that so closely mirrors the cosmic dance of yin and yang as sex. Indeed, if the human species reproduced in a way that involved three people, it is conceivable that the *tai chi tu* (the circular yin/yang symbol, see pages 10–11) might have three "tadpoles" instead of two—with far-reaching implications for philosophers.

Sex is a completely natural expression of love and intimacy, of the mutual yearning of yin and yang (the notion of sex as something shameful or sinful is very much a Judeo-Christian concept). Sex should be treated as a gift of yourself to your loved one, not as something to be squandered; on the other hand, withholding sex as a punishment, or using it as a bribe, is not a good idea either.

Sex should be equally playful and tender, exciting and soothing, enlivening and calming. Enjoy the physical and emotional aspects together.

HOW TO USE THE CRYSTALS

Although it is customary to group crystals in odd numbers (usually three), rather than even numbers, sexual love in particular celebrates the union of two people, so this essential idea of two-ness—of yin and yang—needs to be represented, but without jinxing the affair with a traditionally unlucky pair of crystals. The solution is to position the pair of crystals inside a bowl, or on top of some sort of stand or mat (ideally a circular one). This arrangement provides the traditional third element that embraces the pair within a unifying field of love.

◆ Choose your stones carefully: one represents you, while the other denotes your partner or partner-to-be. Traditionally, red jasper symbolizes stamina and energy (the yang side of the equation), and a massage wand or other cylindrical crystal is ideal to represent the male or more dominant partner. For the female or yin partner, an egg-shaped, round or (better still) crystal with a hole through the middle in rose quartz (for love and tenderness) or pink calcite (for compassionate tolerance) is perfect. You may prefer different crystals—amethyst for fidelity and sobriety, for example, or sugilite for a more spiritual love—but you should try to keep to the suggested shapes if at all possible.

◆ Put your chosen crystals inside the bowl, or on top of your stand or mat. Place this on a windowsill or dressing table, and leave it in full view as long as the relationship lasts. If—or when—it ends, separate the crystals, keeping your own and giving the other away, to symbolize the end of the affair.

◆ If your relationship is going through a phase (as most relationships do) when sex has become dull or mundane, or one or both partners is too tired to be interested, try placing tiger's eye carved into the shape of a heart at the head of the bed; alternatively, you could both wear a small piece of tiger's eye jewelry. Think of your partner when you look at the gemstone. This may also be helpful if you wish to try a little exploration in sexual matters—but always take care not to cause harm, remembering that not everyone is supple enough for all the positions in the *Kama Sutra*.

PARTNERSHIP

Crystals for partnerships are a little different from sex crystals. Sex may still be a part of the relationship, but partnership is a somewhat more complex matter than a straightforward physical liaison.

Partnership involves compromise and reliance on the other person. It can be as much spiritual and intellectual as it is physical and emotional. It requires commitment, trust, and honesty. At its best, partnership is the union of two people who nevertheless retain their unique individuality, who are a haven for each other and who share the burdens and tribulations of life together. Such a complete partnership is uncommon, but there's no reason why you shouldn't aim for it.

It's important to be clear about what both sides want from the partnership, so good communication is vital. It sounds obvious, but it's surprising how easy it can be not to take the time to talk to each other. Make such discussion a regular event, too, because your needs and desires will change over time and some aspects of the partnership may need realigning.

A loving partnership is one of the most precious gifts life can give us, something to be cherished and prized.

TWO-CRYSTAL PARTNERSHIP

There's no denying that partnerships entail considerable work, from both of those involved, and there's no substitute for the necessary effort. However, you can give your relationship a boost with this crystal exercise, which encourages you to think clearly about what you want and what you are trying to achieve.

♦ You and your partner both need to choose a crystal that represents yourself. You should do this alone so that you cannot influence each other's choice. The crystals should be pink, purple, or yellow, but within these constraints they can be any shade you like, as long as they symbolize you and the way you feel about yourself.

♦ Place the crystals side by side and consider how they contrast or harmonize with one another—this can give you a fascinating insight into your partner's view of himself or herself, and may even indicate possible hitches to come (if one crystal is disproportionately large, for example, it may suggest that this person sees himself or herself as the more prominent member of the partnership, which could ultimately cause friction in the relationship).

♦ You now need to "bind" the two crystals together. Use pink embroidery silk, or a fine golden chain, to join the two, tying it carefully around both crystals, but leaving a small amount of slack between them—after all, you don't want to strangle the relationship.

♦ Sit the crystals upright in a small bowl half-filled with sand or stone chips, preferably with their bases together, making a "V for victory" shape: partnership is as much about facing the world together as it is about love between two people.

♦ Put the bowl on a sunny windowsill in the bedroom, or where the light will catch it, and spare a moment to consider its significance every time you catch sight of it.

♦ A variation on this exercise is to choose your partner's crystal, and get your partner to pick your crystal. Seeing a crystal expression of how your partner perceives you can be most enlightening!

THE GIFT OF **FRIENDSHIP**

It has been said many times that your friends are the family you choose for yourself. They come in all shapes, sizes, and ages; some may be like-minded, while others will hold ideas quite opposite to your own. Whatever the case, these are the people that you turn to in order to enrich your life, and to share your greatest triumphs and disasters.

Friends are precious. They deserve to be treated with dignity, courtesy, and respect, although all too often they are taken for granted—not necessarily deliberately, but because real friends often seem to be an extension of yourself, both reliable and trustworthy. Now is a good time to reflect on friendship, on your own friends, and on how to be a good friend yourself.

Friends are the gears that make our lives run more smoothly— and the champagne and roses that give our lives sparkle!

CONSOLIDATE A FRIENDSHIP

This little gift-giving exercise not only helps you to develop your own intuition, but strengthens the element of spontaneity in your friendships.

♦ Make yourself comfortable: lying on the bed is a good place.

♦ Hold a crystal in your hand. Double-ended quartz crystals are perfect for this exercise since it concerns two-way communication; naturally pointed crystals are preferable, but artificially shaped stones are satisfactory. Citrine is ideal for developing communication skills, while rose quartz is perfect for promoting warm affection.

♦ Relax and consider the following questions:

What does friendship mean to you? Trust, honesty, someone to listen to you, no matter what you have to say? A mutually beneficial relationship? Someone to lean on, or someone who leans on you?

What sort of friends do you have? One close, intimate friend? A few very good friends? A large circle of casual acquaintants? People who think the same as you? A group with a healthy mix of different opinions and beliefs? Different groups of friends for different occasions? Do you consider your workmates to be friends? What about Internet buddies? You may not be able to speak to them in the flesh, but that doesn't mean that friends made online can't be just as close and important to you as those whom you see every day—and they can often broaden your horizons (social, intellectual, and emotional).

What sort of friend are you? Supportive, caring, reliable, tolerant? Discriminating or patronizing? Do people look up to you, asking for your help and advice? Or do you use your friends, taking advantage of them? Do you choose equals, or people who make you look good? Do you listen as well as talk; talk as well as listen?

♦ Consider what sort of a friend you want yourself to be, and what changes (if any) you need to make in order to become that person.

♦ Start by choosing one or two of your own friends and find them a crystal. Ignore what you may know about the traditional meanings of that crystal and go with your gut

Tumbled rose quartz

Raw citrine

Double-terminated phantom quartz

feelings concerning which crystal best represents the person in question (you can always look up the meanings later on and see how good your instincts were).

♦ Present the crystal to your friend with no more ceremony than a simple, "I saw this and thought of you."

3 KITCHEN
Family and traditions

The kitchen is associated with the element of wood and with the color green. It represents the core of the home, and the family and ancestry that surround you. In this chapter you will discover how crystals in the kitchen can enhance family traditions and togetherness.

CRYSTALS FOR THE KITCHEN:
NOURISHING THE FAMILY

Preparing food is an art enjoyed by many people, but some people fail to find joy in this vital area of life, often because they do not feel at home in their kitchen. Whatever the size or condition of your kitchen, there are practical steps you can take to enhance this important room and make time spent there both happier and safer. When chi can flow freely in the kitchen, there is greater ease of movement, making accidents less likely to happen and less severe if they do occur.

Raw chrysoprase

INSPIRATIONAL KITCHEN CRYSTALS

Although food comes in as many bright and attractive colors as crystals themselves, green is the color traditionally associated with the kitchen. When you consider that vegetation is the basis of virtually your entire diet—either directly, or through animals eating the plants—a light leafy green is a cheerful and appropriate hue to include in your kitchen's color scheme.

Tumbled moss agate

- Chrysoprase is a charming apple-green mineral composed of many tiny crystals; it enjoys a reputation for inspiring tolerance and calm—helpful qualities in the kitchen, given that even professional chefs can become over-excited as they hone their culinary skills. This cooling crystal can really help take the heat out of the accident zone, although a busy kitchen's greasy dust can quickly make chrysoprase look tired.
- Moss agate is an easier crystal to keep clean, and its internal branching structures inspire an awareness of growth, sustainability, and prosperity.

PLACEMENT TIPS

Because the elements of fire and water are mutually destructive, they are best kept separate. If you have fire

Polished green jade

elements (such as a stove or microwave) placed alongside water elements (such as a sink, refrigerator, or dishwasher), they can create tension that leads to a buildup of stress. Tradition suggests that wood is the best insulation between such conflicts, and a green crystal hung or placed between these elements can offer some resolution of the strain.

Another source of stress for the cook is a feeling of vulnerability while working at the stove: the white noise of bubbling saucepans, and attention focused on the cooking food, robs the chef of any notion of what is going on behind him or her. Installing something shiny—such as an agate slice—above the stove will reveal movements behind you and help to promote a sense of being in control. This crystal mirror should in particular reveal anyone who is using the door.

The enjoyment of food is one of the great pleasures of life. Prepared with love, even the simplest meal becomes a feast for the spirit too.

Obesity is a major health issue of the early 21st century, and one of the Chinese art of placement's insights offers a tried-and-tested technique to help dieters. If the kitchen is visible from the front door, then the moment you enter your home, your eye, your thoughts, and your stomach are drawn to the delights that the kitchen holds. If you can't erect a screen or bead curtain incorporating some attractive green crystals, try to position something in the hallway to arrest the eye and distract the mind. Simple solutions range from hanging a crystal cluster to positioning a large crystal or a stone ornament on a shelf just below eye level.

THE HEARTH: **HEART OF THE HOME**

The kitchen produces a regular output of nourishment. It's often called the heart of the home—and the heart of the kitchen is the stove. Originally, of course, the stove was a hearth: a simple affair, like a camp fire or fire pit, with a caldron or spit suspended above it, in which the actual cooking took place, providing warmth for the whole family as well as food. The hearth was central to the life of the household, and allowing the fire there to go out was a sign of bad household management, an uncaring attitude to the welfare of the family, and disastrous bad luck.

While most people these days use electricity or gas to cook on, rather than fire, the attributes of the hearth remain. An uncaring attitude toward diet (both your own and the diet of those whom you are responsible for feeding) leads to a host of ailments and illnesses. While healthy eating can't cure everything, it's an excellent preventative medicine.

To promote prosperity, place a symbol of wealth and abundance between the sunrise and equatorial directions of your kitchen. A green stone bowl (made of serpentine or marble) containing fresh fruit is ideal, but a green crystal in a shape that suggests plenty will suffice—as long as it doesn't add clutter to the room.

The green of growing things and of crystals brings life into the kitchen—useful as well as beautiful and a link to the natural world.

Polished green jade

Tumbled yellow jade

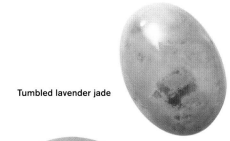

Tumbled lavender jade

Polished blue jade

To ensure that the traditional qualities of the ancient hearth—nourishing food, loving warmth, and family togetherness—are present in your home, construct and empower your own symbolic hearthstone in the kitchen. This exercise is perfect when you are moving into a new home, and it can be repeated yearly, ideally at dawn on the spring equinox, as a reaffirmation of your family spirit.

Jade (both jadeite, which includes the rarer and more expensive "imperial jade," and nephrite) has been valued throughout the ages as a symbol of longevity and ancestral power, treasured by the Mayan and Aztec cultures of Central America, by the Chinese and Japanese, and by the Maoris of New Zealand. Jade artefacts have even been found in prehistoric lake villages in Switzerland. It is a venerable and precious stone (in fact, the Chinese character for "precious" consists of the character for jade repeated twice).

♦ Find a piece of green jade—preferably square or cubic to symbolize the Earth, although any shape will do for this exercise; a jade "palm stone" would be perfectly adequate. The stone should be large enough to be visible from the door of the kitchen, but not so big that it takes up valuable kitchen space.

♦ Now place your jade hearthstone in your kitchen, ideally on the windowsill, but if this isn't possible, then anywhere it can be seen while not getting in the way of normal kitchen activities is fine.

♦ Light a small green candle (an apple-scented one would be perfect) and place it behind the crystal. As it burns, imagine yourself stepping back in time, from today to the distant past: the flame represents the link through time from your most ancient ancestors to yourself, and on into the future.

♦ Let the candle burn for at least half an hour before extinguishing it, taking care that it is positioned safely, with no risk of setting fire to anything; don't leave it burning while you are not in the room.

SOUL FOOD

Food from the hearth sustains your body, but ideas nourish your mind. So many ideas surround us nowadays that you can actually suffer from information overload. And if you can't mentally digest ideas properly, you may become confused and even develop the psychological equivalent of an eating disorder: either starving yourself of essential facts or stuffing your head with trivia and brain-candy. The recipe for a healthy mind is the same as that for a healthy body: a balanced diet and plenty of exercise.

Sometimes you may feel the need to shrug off your burdens and simply dance the night away. The light, almost yellowish-green of prehnite can help to raise your spirits to enable you to see clearly over the rut of oppressive ideas. So long as you awake refreshed, you'll meet life's rewarding challenges with renewed vigor.

FOOD FOR THOUGHT

How you respond to unexpected situations is largely conditioned by your home environment—but your native culture gives you a wardrobe of ready-to-wear crystals to suit almost any event. Chinks in your armor are targeted by unscrupulous advertisers, enticing you to buy things you neither need nor want; slick advertisements may persuade you to make purchases that look fantastic, but your enthusiasm can rapidly turn to dismay when a design flaw ruins your enjoyment.

- Malachite, with its rippling bands of light and dark, reminds you that life is full of ups and downs: while disappointment may plunge you into a dark mood, you can become light-hearted once more by determining not to be fooled again. Developing mental strength will seal those chinks in your psychic armor that are so

Tumbled malachite

Raw dioptase

Raw emerald

readily exploited by confidence tricksters. Displaying malachite in the kitchen, ideally where you can see it while working at the sink, reminds you that even after the dark and barren winter, nature's greenery soon returns as the year brightens.

- Emerald is the crystal of choice for nurturing the inner clarity that is your best guide when exploring different traditions (dioptase crystals are also excellent). Without such an aid, you risk losing your sense of perspective and humor. These crystals prompt you to recognize the goodness and value that exists in other cultures—cultures that grow like facets of a single crystal.

It is especially important to understand the culture you grew up in, for only then can you respect your forebears' achievements and sacrifices, and appreciate the legacy they left you. Such research also inspires compassion for the struggles of other cultures.

As a child, you accepted and trusted your upbringing without question, but you can't stay a child for ever, however hard you might try. Indeed, unless traditional ideas and values can continually pass the test of being relevant to today's needs, they fail and deserve to be replaced. If and when you have children of your own, you will be the elder from whom they instinctively learn, and the authority figure whom they will inevitably question when they too come of age.

The kitchen is an excellent place for us to reaffirm our past—both our own and that of our people.

ANCESTORS AND **SPIRIT GUIDES**

Wise or foolish, tyrannical or kind, your ancestors all had one thing in common: they were successful in passing on their legacy of DNA and achieved a chance of immortality through you. Your genetic history reaches back through the entire history of life on the planet—you even have distant cousins fossilized in limestone and oil.

Many people believe that the spirits of their predecessors continue to watch over them like guardian angels. In fact, the most ancient form of the Chinese art of placement (known as Early Heaven feng shui), which celebrates perfect harmony between nature and the human soul, is still applied to ensure the wellbeing of deceased ancestors, maintaining a relationship between the past and the present.

USEFUL RESEARCH CRYSTALS

You doubtless cherish the memory of those whom you loved, and intuitively know what they would advise you to do, even when you are in a quandary. They may appear in dreams at times of crisis or upheaval, guiding or goading your subconscious mind.

- Green aventurine may help such messages to surface into consciousness—keep it under your pillow, carry it as a charm, or place it on your hearthstone to forge stronger links with your past.
- Green serpentine (ideally richly veined) is particularly helpful to the genealogist, because it promotes lateral thinking. Roots are of vital importance for healthy growth, and there are many ways to trace your roots (if you can't trace your genetic origins, research the history of your present home instead). Sources range from books and official records to the Internet, living relatives and your own memories.

Raw green serpentine

Raw green aventurine

Tumbled moss agate

- Verdite is also useful in historical research, because it promotes perseverance.
- Moss agate (especially mocha stone) has intricate threadlike branches—like the expanding family tree—and is probably the most popular crystal for family historians. It may offer welcome inspiration in your efforts to trace and unravel the riddles of your ancestry. Boost its talismanic powers by storing it with (or even inside) the scroll of your ancestors (see right).

Of course, in a very real sense everyone is immortal: your actions (or inactions) always change your environment, with ripples spreading through space and time—the universe can never be quite the same again.

CREATE A FAMILY SHRINE

The hearthstone in your kitchen offers a clear link to your history and is an ideal location for a family shrine, although it may also be possible to set up a shrine or memorial to your ancestors in the part of your home (or part of a particular room) that faces the pole—your ancestors are like the stars that never set as they circle the celestial pole.

◆ Select a shelf, surface, or even a drawer for your shrine. It may be as elaborate as you wish, with photographs, candles, incense, a bonsai tree, and crystals (such as those mentioned left) placed carefully within it; or as simple as you like.

◆ The key feature is a sheet of green paper, listing the names of your deceased ancestors in a single column. If you run out of room (family history can become very complex), simply tape another sheet of paper to the bottom of the first.

◆ Roll the sheet(s) into a scroll and tie it with red thread, placing it on your shrine. Remembering your ancestors not only helps you to appreciate the world before you were born, but casts a warm and welcome light on your own times.

BALANCING THE **MALE AND FEMALE PRINCIPLES**

Forget the old adage about women being the weaker sex. In the real world, the female principle is tough, enduring, nurturing, and creative. It bestows a steady strength, immense stamina, and a high pain threshold. It also confers a fiercely protective spirit—push it too far and it will push back, many times more strongly. In contrast, the male principle is competitive, aggressive, and explosive. It is sporadically energetic and prone to bursts of great strength, followed by periods of lassitude. It imparts the will to innovate, build, and develop.

Everyone contains elements of yin (the female principle) and yang (the male principle), in varying proportions. Rarely are these proportions equal, and so, instinctively seeking balance in life, people tend to look for a partner who complements their own nature—hence the sayings "Opposites attract" and "My other half."

Finding a measure of harmony within yourself is, however, both possible and desirable; it makes you self-reliant and self-confident, more able to face the problems and challenges of life. It helps to give you a measure of control over yourself and your circumstances. Faceted peridot, a lively and inspirational crystal, is an excellent talisman for this purpose, when worn as earrings or in a ring.

Never be afraid to experiment in the kitchen, as in life.
Take pleasure in the doing as well as the result.

CHANGE YOUR KITCHEN HABITS

To get in touch with the other half of your being, try to alter your culinary habits for a day and look at life from a different perspective. This can be quite therapeutic, so aim to repeat this exercise every now and then.

♦ Put some polished amazonite in plain view in your kitchen: its steady, grounding effect will be very useful as you renovate your lifestyle.

♦ If you usually spend as little time as possible in the kitchen, schedule in a half-day to learn something new: either a new recipe or a fresh way of making an old favorite. Spend some time considering exactly where all the ingredients have come from, how they reached you, how they were grown, and their nutritional value. Knowledge is a major key in gaining control of your life; knowing what makes your body work at its best is a great start in understanding how to make changes within yourself.

♦ Alternatively, if you usually spend a lot of time in the kitchen preparing fresh food, spend one day cooking only "instant" or "junk" food. You might not enjoy the taste very much, but make a point of doing something different and enjoyable with the time that you save.

♦ Don't forget that feeding the spirit is at least as important as feeding the body. Just as food replenishes the body, so the beautiful green stone malachite traditionally refreshes the spirit. A carved malachite dragon makes an ideal talisman, symbolizing healthy energy, new growth, and the vigor of spring. Let it fill your kitchen with vitality.

Tumbled malachite **Raw amazonite**

A CELEBRATION OF **BELONGING**

It doesn't matter how solitary and self-contained a person you are, you still belong to the human race. And everyone is interconnected, sharing responsibility for each other, just as air, water, and DNA are shared with everyone else on the planet. You cannot do anything in this life without affecting countless other people. So it makes sense to consider the effects of your actions before you take them.

The idea behind this celebration of belonging is very simple, ancient, and venerable: a meal with friends, family, and/or colleagues, in your own home, prepared by you (see also pages 130–131 for crystals to use in the living/dining room).

The exuberant joy of sharing the good things in life can be an end in itself and a source of immense satisfaction.

HOW TO PREPARE YOUR CELEBRATION

Your celebration meal can be as simple or as elaborate as you wish—although simpler may be better, because the focus of this exercise is on the people, not the quality or quantity of the food. You can hold the celebration at any time of day (whatever is most convenient for all those involved): coffee and home-made cakes, Sunday brunch or even a summer barbecue—all are equally valid.

♦ The perfect symbol for this exercise are the tortoises of harmony, which can be made of any green stone. They represent family unity—in this case, the unity of the whole human family. They also attract good fortune and health. A stone bowl (symbolic of plenty) made of green fluorite or soapstone is also excellent. Use it to store fruit in, placing it somewhere in the kitchen that you call your own.

♦ Write down the names of all the people you know, or with whom you regularly come into contact. If you don't know their names, jot down reminders of who they are: you may not be on first-name terms with those you see regularly behind store counters, but if you exchange a hello and a smile when you meet, include them on your list. When you've finished, imagine how much poorer your life would be without them all.

♦ Now consider how you would treat them if today were the last day of your life. You wouldn't be human if there weren't a few people you'd like to tell exactly what you think of them, but for the purposes of this exercise, focus on the positive aspects. How many of them would you like to thank—for their friendship, their help, their business, or for generally making life more pleasant for you? Do you owe anything to any of them: time, money, favors, something you've borrowed and forgotten to give back? Can you rectify any of this now?

♦ Ideally, your celebration should include individuals from all races, genders, ages, and walks of life, although in practice that may be impossible. Do your best, though—if you have friends with children, include the youngsters in the invitation; and get your own parents and grandparents to come along, if they can make it.

♦ Gear the event to the size of your kitchen: if it's tiny, don't invite so many people that you all feel claustrophobic. If you don't have room to eat in the kitchen, at least get everyone to assemble there to start with, collecting their drinks, if nothing else, so that you focus on this heart of the home with its associations with family and tradition.

♦ Enjoy each other's company. As you eat your meal, celebrate your differences, your similarities, and the warmth and security of belonging.

4 THE HOME OFFICE
Prosperity

The home office is associated with the element of wood and with the colors green and red, as well as their combinations: brown and reddish-purple. In this chapter you will find suggestions for using crystals in this room to help bring you financial success and good luck in business.

CRYSTALS FOR THE OFFICE:
CREATING A MONEY SPACE

Few people are fortunate enough to earn their living doing something they really love, so it is very important at least to feel comfortable while you are at work. You need to strike a careful balance, however: if you make yourself too comfortable, you will relax too much and become unproductive. You need a secure, yet stimulating space in which you can feel alert enough to dream up new ideas and create fresh financial opportunities.

An efficient office or home-working environment needs the yang of busy activity to be in harmony with the yin of a cool, collected long-term vision. Frenetic action always burns out quickly, leaving your dreams in ashes; similarly, too much planning and insufficient action will get you nowhere. When action and planning are yoked together and working toward the same goal, your enterprise will prosper, albeit in cycles of expansion and contraction—cycles as natural as breathing.

EMPOWERING OBJECTS FOR THE HOME OFFICE

Ideal crystals for this room, which is dedicated to the acquisition of wealth as a means of self-empowerment, combine the red hues of the yang element of fire with the green hues of the yin element of wood.

- Bloodstone (also known as heliotrope) is a popular mineral that symbolizes both inherited wealth and the earned wealth that keeps a family prosperous. Traditionally, bloodstone helps to remove obstacles and promotes dedication and determination.
- Serpentine, with its veins and mottled hues of red and green, can stimulate you to negotiate change, and can even help you to overcome the stress of apparent failure. The patterns in this crystal have long been associated with snakeskin (hence its name), reminding you of your innate ability to free yourself

Raw serpentine

Red jasper polished egg

Tumbled bloodstone

If you have an aquarium in the office, be sure to keep an odd number of fish—odd numbers are luckier than even.

from one situation and start afresh in a new one, just as the serpent (emblem of wisdom) sheds its skin periodically.

- An aquarium is often recommended as a traditional Chinese fix for enhancing the wealth-attracting qualities of an office. However, unless you can offer the fish an excellent habitat, you might do better to install an indoor fountain. This can be sprinkled with an opulent streambed of any red and green crystals; it also acts as a humidifier to help counteract the dry and ionized air produced by computers and other electrical equipment in the home office.

- A reflective crystal, such as an agate slice (placed strategically on your desk so that you can see when somebody enters your workspace), is useful if you sit in a position where you cannot see the door.

- A jade (or money) plant (*Crassula argentea*) can grow fairly large, inspiring your business activities to grow. Cover the soil with polished stones of red jasper to promote a strong competitive edge, stamina, and strength of will. Keep these stones clean and, as you polish them, focus your mind on your intention to sharpen your wits and make steady progress toward success and prosperity. This plant should thrive in light coming from the direction between the sunrise and the equator, the quadrant that is associated with wealth. Tradition maintains that any of the above crystals located in that position—your money space—will gather wealth-producing influences to help you succeed in life.

ACQUIRE **WEALTH**

If you work from home you'll already have a space—a room or part of one—set up for your purposes. If you work elsewhere, find the corner of your desk or office that lies between the directions of the sunrise and the equator, and dedicate it to the acquisition of wealth: this is your "money space." It is also the area of your house that you should use if you don't yet have a home office.

One crystal no office should be without is a "crystal ball"—a small crystal sphere—to promote good fortune and far-sightedness in business. It doesn't have to be large, but it should be placed on a stand so that it doesn't roll around (which would represent instability). Ideally it should be of green and/or purple fluorite, and if possible placed near the phone for success in communication at a distance (see also pages 68–69).

One of the great joys of working for yourself is that you are not concerned solely with profit. With no need to justify your actions to shareholders, you are free to pursue the work that brings you most personal satisfaction—and this is why many people are opting to downsize, so that the pressures on them are fewer. For an employee, this might mean leaving a well-paid but overly stressful job in favor of taking up a post with a less demanding or more flexible company.

Ignoring a lucrative opportunity may seem like madness, but few people actually see money as an end in itself—if you are comfortable and financially secure, then you may prefer to relax a little and enjoy the fruits of your labors. After all, there is little use acquiring wealth unless you can find or make the time to enjoy it.

Fluorite crystal ball

Making a gem tree is a good way of exercising your artistic talents, meditating on your options, and attracting wealth. It also makes an attractive ornament, representing growth, endurance, and fruitfulness. Gem-tree kits are available, but it is more rewarding to make your own tree from scratch. The materials are relatively easy to find in crystal and craft stores.

You will need:

- Gold-colored wire (24-gauge wire is appropriate) for creating the branches
- A large, flat-bottomed crystal (rock quartz is ideal)
- A piece of wood (driftwood or dried wood) to form the trunk
- Quick-drying glue
- Assorted small green crystals (such as aventurine, amazonite, and green serpentine) and red crystals (such as carnelian, garnet, and red tiger's eye)
- Bellcaps or spiral findings (fixing methods) for larger crystals (optional)

◆ Decide on the shape of tree you want: upright for progress; spreading for protection; rounded for prosperity. Don't make a gem tree that looks spiky, if other people will be sitting nearby—clients in particular may feel uneasy with sharp objects pointing at them.

◆ Wrap some gold wire around the large crystal that forms the base and spiraling up the trunk—as many strands as you want branches. Bend them into shape.

◆ Now glue the crystals in place. Use green crystal chips for leaves, and larger red crystals for fruit. Use bellcaps or spiral findings as necessary to help secure the crystals in position.

◆ As you work, focus on your finances.

◆ Once you have finished, place the gem tree in an appropriate position in your home office.

BRANCH **OUT**

Unless you're born or marry into money, or win a large amount on the lottery, you will probably have to find some way to earn the money necessary for survival—hopefully a worthwhile occupation in which you can take pride, even if only in the thought that you are helping others in some way.

Your choice of occupation was probably made at an early age, before you had the chance to experience much of the world. Later you may have felt that your choice was inappropriate, or that your needs and wishes changed as you grew older. It's therefore important to be versatile, and to take the time every now and again to consider both how you want your working life to proceed and exactly what you have to offer. You can place charoite beside your bed (or beneath your pillow) to inspire dreams that may help you to break out of a rut.

Think laterally. Is job satisfaction more important to you than salary? Do you thrive on pressure, or would a low-stress job be better for you? Do you see work as a way to pay for your preferred lifestyle, or as a means of personal fullfilment and satisfaction? Don't view your career as a ladder—it is a web, with interconnecting strands. A sideways move may enrich your life much more than a step upward.

Tumbled ametrine

Tumbled bloodstone

Tumbled charoite

Raw green kunzite

USE CRYSTALS TO TAKE STOCK OF YOUR CAREER

Are you happy with what you do? You spend a large proportion of your life working in one way or another. While not everyone can fulfill their dreams regarding their career, it's very important for your self-esteem and mental health that you gain some fulfillment from your work. To do this you can either make the most of what you have, or initiate some changes in your working life.

♦ First, consider what resources you already possess: your skills, talents, qualifications, and training. Are you over-qualified for your present job? If so, but you're happy, it probably doesn't matter. If not, what opportunities are there for you to use what you have learned? Would a short training course bring you up to date and fit you for a position that's more suitable for you?

♦ What choices are available to you? What opportunities are there close to where you live? Could you move elsewhere to work at something you really enjoy?

♦ What are your responsibilities? If you have a family, certain restrictions will apply, but it should still be possible to balance your domestic affairs with a satisfying job, even if it takes a little ingenuity. Perhaps working from home would be a good move for you. Kunzite, a lilac or purple transparent crystal, traditionally promotes self-discipline and responsibility, both qualities that are vital for success in this situation. Keep it in your workspace.

♦ Now try using the following crystals to enhance your working life. Bloodstone, a dark-green crystal speckled with red, has a long tradition of demolishing barriers and opening doors, while ametrine promotes flashes of inspiration. Both are ideal to wear or hold when taking stock and making decisions about your career. Carry a small, smooth crystal with you, perhaps in the form of jewelry, when you are at work, or keep a palm-sized piece in your home office.

♦ It is also useful to keep readily to hand a red and green serpentine "worry-egg" (an egg-shaped crystal that you knead in your hands to relieve tension), to help soothe away the stresses and strains of inducing wide-ranging changes to your lifestyle.

STEPPING STONES TO **SUCCESS**

Working smarter is all about making the most of your resources, and your single most valuable resource is probably your time.

Thinking ahead can pay dividends. For example, if you need extra qualifications to pursue your chosen career, finding the time (or place) to study can be a real challenge, and you may need to make careful adjustments to your lifestyle first. Trusting to luck can sometimes work, but planning ahead gives you the confidence to enjoy the journey. Your spirit may, in a single leap of faith, bridge the gulf between actuality and your dreams, but your physical body must take things one step at a time, so you need to create stepping stones on the path to success.

A tidy, clean, and easily accessible work-space is vital for efficient working– but it must also be comfortable for the person using it.

CREATE A CRYSTAL CHART

Using just a sheet of card and five crystals (small, polished specimens are fine), you can make a plan: not a map of the physical space around you, but a chart of your future.

♦ At the top of the sheet of card, write a list of keywords about what you would like to be doing in, say, ten years' time. Now select a crystal to represent this goal—any crystal will do (and this book is full of suggestions), but red ones (such as carnelian or red aventurine) symbolize strength, stamina, determination, and passion and are general-purpose stand-ins. The crystals suggested below in parentheses may be considered traditional (their colors are related to the central column of the *lo shu*), but always try to make your own choice of crystal. Then place the crystal on your list.

♦ At the bottom of the sheet write a few descriptive words about what you are doing now. Choose another crystal (such as black onyx or obsidian) to place on top of this.

♦ At the midpoint between these crystals, write notes about the sorts of things you might be doing halfway to your dreams coming true. Place a crystal (such as citrine or yellow amber) here.

♦ As you were focusing on the central crystal, you probably also thought of some intermediate stages or events linking this central phase with the top or bottom phases. Make notes for the phase between the middle and top, in the space left between them. Place a crystal (such as pale carnelian or amber) here.

♦ Finally consider the lower transition, and record your ideas carefully between the central and bottom phases. Place a crystal (such as tiger's eye or brown jasper) here.

♦ Now position this chart securely in your home office or money space, as a sort of shrine to future prosperity, where you can handle the crystals as you periodically meditate on each phase of making your dreams come true. A photograph of the chart pinned to a memo board can work as well, enabling you to recycle the crystals when creating new charts.

♦ It is particularly important to explore in great detail the route you need to take between where you are now and the next phase—and making a new chart is an ideal method. The last crystal you placed on the original chart becomes the first (topmost) crystal of your new chart. Then you simply fill in the gaps as before, working out all the stepping stones that will lead you along your chosen path.

♦ Create as many charts as you wish, exploring a range of possible futures, both for yourself and for your loved ones.

Tumbled tiger's eye

Raw citrine

Raw red aventurine

Tumbled black onyx

Polished amber

GENEROSITY

There are calls on your generosity every day–people, charities, and organizations pleading with you to part with your money. They range from the homeless person begging in the street to credit-card companies trying to attract your allegiance by donating a proportion of their profits to specific charities. There's no shortage of good causes, from the small and local to the huge and global. And donations range from small regular payments, automatically deducted from your bank account, to spontaneous giving in the wake of natural disasters.

Generosity isn't solely to do with giving money–in fact, one could say that cash is the easy option (especially if you have plenty to start with). Donating items such as clothing, kitchenware, or books to charity stores requires a little more thought and effort. But the hardest–yet most rewarding–gift is something personally valuable, such as your time or expertise. Consider carrying an organ-donor card or becoming a blood-donor: both take very little effort on your part, but are literally life-savers for other people. True generosity gives without asking or expecting anything in return.

Take a moment to consider your favorite and least favorite charities (if you don't have any, choose them now). Why do you–or would you–support them? Have they benefited you or someone you know? How can you do more to help them? Can you volunteer to help out in a store, or by collecting, giving your time or campaigning for them?

Cultivate a generous spirit. This doesn't mean emptying your billfold into every collecting box you encounter (unless you want to and can afford it, of course), but offering help to those who need it. Even the simplest act can brighten the world for someone else. There are numerous anecdotes testifying to the fact that the generosity you give somehow returns to you when you most need it, and while this is never a reason to be generous, there's no harm in bearing it in mind.

Polished watermelon tourmaline

Banded fluorite wand

THE ROLE OF CRYSTALS

Crystals won't change the world you live in, or even your intentions, but they can remind you of the benefits of generosity.

- Banded fluorite, a beautiful transparent crystal with bands ranging from green to purple, supports you in your efforts to move resources where they are most needed. If you can find a banded fluorite sphere, so much the better: place it near the phone in your home office to enhance two-way communication. Altruism is a noble ideal, and if you can benefit more than one person or cause— including yourself—by your actions, you will be making better use of your own resources.

- Watermelon tourmaline, with its warm red heart and fertility-green encircling outer layer, is perfect for reminding you to nurture those in need; and, in so doing, you strengthen your own humanity. Keep a small piece with your cash and/or in your billfold.

A crystal ball won't reveal the future, but positioned by the telephone it can remind us to consider the needs of others as well as our own.

LUCK

Are you born lucky or can luck be acquired? The answer is a little of both. The Chinese believe there are actually three kinds of luck: the luck you're born with, the luck you make for yourself, and the luck that comes to you from your environment. You can't do much about the first, but you can certainly influence the last two.

CRYSTAL ANIMALS FOR GOOD FORTUNE

Crystals by themselves will not make you lucky, but a variety of crystal objects are traditionally placed in the home office or money space to attract wealth and luck. Many people also carry some sort of mascot, or amulet, to attract good luck.

- The hare or rabbit is a surprisingly common charm. Perhaps because it is so widespread and so difficult to eradicate, this animal has come to symbolize the overcoming of all odds—and hence success and good fortune. The rabbit is a popular subject for crystal carving, so finding one you like should not prove difficult. Red and green serpentine, banded fluorite, and bloodstone are ideal crystals. If the object is small enough, carry it with you; otherwise keep it in your workspace, where you can handle it frequently so that the good luck can "rub off" on you.

- A crystal frog or toad is a symbol of abundance, and is often placed on a small pile of coins (Chinese "cash" coins are perfect for this purpose) in your money space to generate income. Unakite fosters realism and a sense of perspective along with a good-humored attitude to work, making it perfect for this talisman.

- A bloodstone dragon pendant, bracelet, or ring can easily be incorporated into your daily life. Wearing amulets as jewelry has a long and venerable history, and can be very attractive.

- You could also try keeping carved crystals in the following forms:
  A fish (preferably a carp) for riches.
  An elephant to boost intelligence and bring good fortune in exams.
  A gourd for long life.
  Fu dogs for protection and to promote valor and prosperity.
  A dragon for protection and all-round good luck.
  A cicada to transform bad luck into good.
  A horse for luck with lotteries.

GAMBLING

Gambling disrupts the natural flow of chi. Obviously the occasional "flutter" isn't going to be disastrous, but it can become an addiction if it is not kept under control. Gambling anything—your health, wealth, or happiness—is a sure way of generating bad luck. It upsets the balance of yin and yang, and although you may be successful for a little while, eventually the balance will swing back in the other direction, resulting in a stream of negative energy and a run of bad luck.

Sometimes you may need help keeping your feet on the ground and remembering that luck—good or bad—is always temporary. Red and green serpentine (the more richly crazed with veins, the better) can act as a powerful talisman to help keep a sense of perspective.

Banded fluorite wand

Tumbled bloodstone

Raw red and green serpentine

A unakite frog on three cash coins—the ideal talisman for generating a steady flow of money-generating work.

5 HOME SANCTUARY
Harmony, wellbeing, and health

This room of the home is associated with the element of earth and with the color yellow. It represents the nucleus, and is associated with balance and wellbeing. In this chapter you will learn how to use crystals to create a "place of your own" at home, in which to nurture your health and a rich spiritual life.

CRYSTALS FOR YOUR
HOME SANCTUARY

Positioned at the very heart of the *lo shu* grid of the home (see pages 14–15), this chamber represents the point of perfect balance between every aspect of your life. The other eight rooms surround the hub of the sanctuary like petals, and here in the nucleus you should feel most at home and in tune with the strength and potential of the universe.

Few people have a temple or meditation room in their homes, but everyone has a favorite place. For many it's simply the bed; for others it's the study, or perhaps a den, lounge, or the garden.

Because this space is intimately connected with the other eight rooms, you may wish to work through the remaining chapters before introducing crystal changes to your home sanctuary. Any sanctuary is better than none, and so, if you don't yet have a dedicated place in your home where you can just *be*, try some of the simpler ideas in this chapter first. Staurolite with crystals in a cross shape, and chiastolite, are both wonderful symbols of the sanctuary, cherished by beginners and experts alike. Either can help focus your mind on creating or improving your sanctuary.

Chiastolite slice

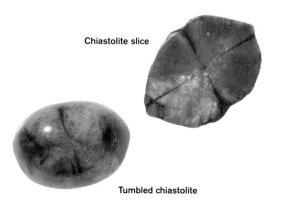

Tumbled chiastolite

FIND YOUR HEART CRYSTAL

Just as each person is at the center of his or her individual world, so selecting a crystal to place at the heart of your special space, your sanctuary, is a very personal experience. Your heart crystal is a reflection of yourself and can reveal aspects of you that are rarely glimpsed otherwise—insights that may take years to develop clearly. So view your heart crystal often, and from all sides.

Your stone (it needn't be a crystal in the strict sense) is an embodiment of you and may incorporate a wide range of aspects that make it uniquely attractive to you. It may not be easy to find such an intimate crystal companion, and your search may come to resemble a quest, but there is much to be gained from the mere act of seeking.

- Ensure you are familiar with the advice on choosing crystals (see pages 8–9).

- Set a budget you can afford.

- Tidy your sanctuary in readiness to receive your new crystal.

- Don't look for a crystal to help you in a particular aspect of your life. Seek one that inspires you with its beauty.

- Don't simply buy the crystal you want—buy the one you can't leave behind.

- Introduce it to your home carefully, and with a sense of occasion, as if bringing home a long-lost sibling.

- Position it with care in your sanctuary, and photograph it as a permanent reminder of the moment.

- Note and record every time you move your heart crystal—each move may mirror a significant change in your life, such as branching out in a new career or changing a key personal relationship.

- Everyone develops and evolves, so don't be surprised if you have a succession of different heart crystals, each of which is special to that moment in time.

A LITTLE **PARADISE**

The word "paradise" originally referred to an enclosure or park, and gradually came to mean a walled garden; its later identification with heaven gave it the added connotation of a beautiful, secluded, sacred place, a sanctuary.

Gardens hold a very special appeal to many of us. From the grandest of public estates to a tiny rooftop refuge with plants in pots, this living, breathing space represents a haven, somewhere you can go to touch the natural world for a while.

What does the term "garden" mean to you? A square of grass where you can sunbathe? A plot where you can grow vegetables? Somewhere for the children to play in safety? A formal garden with carefully pruned and maintained shrubs and flowerbeds, or a natural wildlife garden full of native flowers, insects, and small animals?

A garden fills all the senses, soothes the mind and the body, and allows us time and space to commune with our inner selves.

CREATE A GARDEN AS SANCTUARY

A garden is never truly finished. It grows and changes over the years—just as you do—displaying different aspects of its beauty in different seasons. Take time to enjoy its many aspects, in whatever form they take for you.

♦ Plan your ideal garden: include everything you can think of, from favorite plants and features to paths and seating areas. Include some rocks and stones in a variety of colors— these are crystals just as much as those inside the home— but be sure you buy them from a reputable source and don't lift them from the natural landscape. How much is possible in your own garden, given your space and financial constraints? How much of it could you do yourself, and how much would need to be done by a professional gardener? Consider whether you are prepared to put in the necessary work to maintain it.

♦ If you don't have an outdoor garden, or would like another one, plan to create one indoors. There is a huge range of indoor plants to choose from, ranging from those that are expensive and harder to care for (such as orchids) to cheap and easy-care varieties. There are even a few plants, such as aspidistras, that thrive on neglect. Find out which plants will do best in which rooms: cacti, succulents, and most flowering pot-plants will do well on sunny windowsills, while ferns will prefer shady areas. Include one large, tall plant, if at all possible; it brings the forest into your home. Place moss agates on the soil around the plants, because this crystal fosters strong growth.

♦ If you cannot manage even a pot-plant in your home, at least obtain or make a miniature Zen garden: the sand and stones represent water and mountains, and act to focus the mind on the larger world outside. Use yellow or white sand and citrine and tiger's eye crystals instead of rocks, and keep your garden in the space you've designated as your

Tumbled tiger's eye

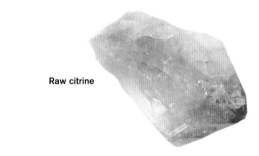

Raw citrine

Tumbled moss agate

sanctuary. The act of slowly and carefully raking the sand into flowing patterns calms the mind and spirit, while contemplating the simple serenity of the miniature landscape is soothing and reenergizing—a powerful way of rebalancing chi.

HEALTH, HEALING, AND **WELLBEING**

Your wellbeing depends on a number of factors: healthy eating, sensible exercise, sufficient sleep, moderation when it comes to the enjoyable things that really aren't good for you—alcohol, chocolate, sugary treats—and a positive mental attitude. You can't change your heredity, and some inherited physical conditions can't be overcome, but you can take steps to improve your health and your quality of life.

A healthy body is one of life's great pleasures. To move easily, to sit and lie without pain, to have enough energy to enjoy life, and to sleep comfortably and soundly—these are everyone's fundamental rights. Unfortunately the stresses and temptations of modern life often have a decidedly negative effect, one that you can usually see when you look in the mirror.

Striving for perfection is admirable, as long as you understand that perfection is by definition unattainable, and as long as you don't become depressed when you fall short of that goal. If you have done what you can to improve your overall lifestyle, you can be confident that your body will respond, although the changes will be gradual. You aren't trying for a quick fix, but for changes that will enhance every aspect of your life.

Note that none of this advice is intended to replace conventional medical care: if you have any health concerns, always see a doctor.

MEDITATION FOR POSITIVE THINKING

Meditation soothes and calms the mind, enabling you to perceive things more clearly. It is an excellent way to "fix" a positive mental outlook that will help you to stay vigorous and dynamic throughout life. In theory, meditation is easy, but the practice can prove a little more difficult. However, it's not necessary to learn how to empty your mind completely; you can gain considerable benefit from a less intense form of meditation.

♦ Prepare your sanctuary, making it as comfortable as you possibly can.

♦ Choose an appropriate crystal as a focus for your meditation: your heart crystal (see pages 74–75) is ideal; or rutilated quartz, which boosts energy and promotes youthfulness and the body's defense systems. Your Zen garden (see pages 76–77) is another excellent focal point, as is the Early Heaven *ba gua*, a Chinese mandala (or circular design) of spiritual harmony. Contemplating this promotes calm and wellbeing as your eyes meander along its balanced pattern of yin (- -) and yang (−).

The Early Heaven *ba gua*.

♦ Gaze at your chosen focus, letting your eyes–and your mind–follow the shapes and patterns within it. Breathe deeply and slowly, feeling your body relax. Smile: this will automatically make you feel happier, as well as being kinder to your face than a frown.

♦ Imagine yourself feeling in perfect health, happy, fit, and strong. Feel the chi flowing through your body, filling you with energy, swirling around you, protective and healing. Imagine yourself surrounded by a golden light, warm and gentle, infusing you with contentment.

♦ Remember that feeling. After a few meditations you should be able to call it up at any time you wish, and use it to give you the strength and energy to deal with whatever problems are at hand.

Tumbled rutilated quartz

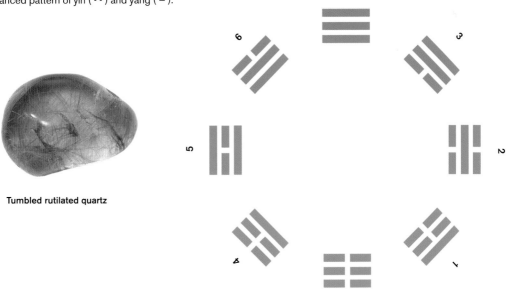

COMPLETION AND **BALANCE**

Within your sanctuary you can be wholly and simply yourself. There is no one here to criticize you for your faults or to condemn you for your shortcomings. Here you can safely confront the things you don't like about yourself, admitting your fears and fantasies without embarrassment or compromise. Everyone has flaws, and while you may hide or disguise them from others, acknowledging them to yourself means that you can take steps to deal with them.

The grid pattern of the *lo shu* reflects the ancient Chinese pictogram (or picture symbol) *jing*: a well surrounded by eight plots of land. Just as the entire community was sustained by this vital, central water source, so your sanctuary can become a wellspring of fertility refreshing every facet of your life, every day.

Tumbled rose quartz

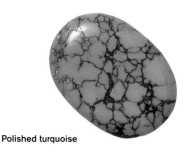

Polished turquoise

ANALYZE YOURSELF

Before you can deal with your flaws, you have to face them. Try this exercise to assess who you are and what you can learn from your own shortcomings.

♦ Make time to be alone and undisturbed. Ensure that you're neither hungry nor over-full, and have a drink nearby.

♦ Make yourself comfortable, then meditate for a while (see pages 78–79), but this time use either your heart crystal or a piece of opal (preferably black opal)–this beautiful crystal symbolizes both truth and inner mysteries, and gazing into its shimmering, shifting play of colors assists introspection. Once you are feeling relaxed, calm, and positive, turn your attention inward.

♦ Now ask yourself the follow questions:

Who are you: what is the real you, the sum of all your experiences, fears, hopes, and dreams? How do you perceive yourself? Do you like who you are?

What motivates you? Love, fear, envy, anger? Why? Are you satisfied with your answers?

What do you fear most deeply? Do you know why?

What would be the ideal you? How can you change to more closely resemble that ideal?

♦ Honesty is vital in this exercise–as is realism. The ultimate aim is to feel content within yourself, confident that you have done the best you can to fulfill your potential, without hurting anyone else along the way. It may sound like a modest goal, but it's attainable for everyone and will result in happiness, rather than the frustration and sense of failure that accompany trying to achieve the impossible.

♦ It's important not to come away from the exercise feeling depressed. Never forget that, no matter how glaring or

dreadful your own faults and flaws might seem, they are part of what makes you yourself, and are valuable as an insight into your personality. They aren't "bad" or "evil" in themselves—they balance the positive chi of your inner self. And remember that everyone has shortcomings, some of them far worse than yours. You are not alone in being human!

♦ Take a little time to think about what you have learned about yourself. Are you satisfied with who you are? If so, celebrate! If you aren't, celebrate anyway: you've appraised yourself, accepted that there are changes you want to make, and now have the excitement of discovering how to best make your desired improvements.

Tumbled amethyst

CRYSTAL **DIVINATION**

People have always had a fascination with consulting fortune tellers. Oracles may be as simple as a coin tossed for a yes/no decision, as complex as astrology, or as intuitive as dream interpretation. Divination offers insights, like visions seen in a crystal sphere, but rarely certainties. Our free will is not subjugated by any forecast, yet a true oracle offers a valuable chance to prepare for the challenge of change.

CONSULT THE CRYSTAL ORACLE

This simple, yet powerful system aims to stimulate your subconscious into understanding your situation, rather than merely predicting events. Write a record of your consultations, in order to check your accuracy and progress.

◆ Select a crystal with a pointed end: a small quartz wand is fine, but a rounded, polished tiger's eye is ideal.

◆ Shake the crystal in cupped hands and concentrate on your chosen question, then let the crystal fall onto a soft surface (such as a napkin or carpet).

◆ If the crystal points toward or away from you, draw a horizontal line. If it points to either side, draw a pair of shorter lines beside each other (like two horizontal lines with a gap in the middle).

◆ Cast your crystal again and, higher up on your page, draw the resulting line or pair of lines.

◆ Cast the crystal a third and final time, and draw the result in the space between the other records.

◆ If you can't tell which sort of line is indicated, repeat the cast, but expect the interpretation to be quite hard to understand.

◆ There are eight different possible interpretations, as described opposite.

Stable as the Earth

Even a hopeless situation can turn to long-term advantage if you open your heart to a break with the past. The void may be a dreamless sleep before awakening—be receptive to the next wave as it rises.

High as a mountain

Watch and learn, and put your observations to good use later. Plan a venture, study, write a novel, or seek that mystical moment when you achieve an overview of your life—then pass through the portal.

Flowing like water

Life may seem like a gushing river sweeping you along. Just beyond the banks, though, everything remains unmoved. The moon shines in the heart of the night—a beacon and guide to the mind's eye.

Chaotic as the wind

Change is all around—rediscover your surroundings. The key to a difficult situation may lie in your own hands. Great opportunities can arise in the least expected places: truth is a lover without shame.

Irresistible as an earthquake

Everyone must move with the times, but weigh the outcome with care. Allow deep-seated doubts to gently nag their way into full consciousness: "sleep on it" before taking an irrevocable departure.

Energetic as fire

Release your enthusiasm and confidence, and express your inner feelings: a friend may become a lover; or a spontaneous weekend break could be the holiday of a lifetime. Explore beyond the horizons.

Peaceful as a lake

Like still waters in a deep valley, rest and settle yourself. Gather your wits and do not instantly react to every tempting offer. Even in a storm your heart can remain at peace and see its way clearly.

Whole as heaven

The fruits of labor are ripe and ready for the taking. The stage is set for festivities and joy in an environment of unity and goodwill, and a powerful burst of undiluted energy can be achieved.

THE SANCTUARY AS **HAVEN**

Your sanctuary is your refuge. It gives you your sense of place, a feeling of belonging. It's an outward expression of your inner self, and somewhere you feel safe. You may, if you wish, embellish it with a small shrine—this might be particularly appealing if others share the space, or part of it (for instance, if the family garden or den is also your sanctuary).

The shrine should be yours alone; no one else should touch it or move any of its component parts without your permission. It may therefore be useful to create a shrine that can be put together and disassembled easily, whenever you wish, perhaps stored in a special box acquired specifically for that purpose. You might choose to do this anyway, even if you have a permanent sanctuary. In order to remain healthy, chi must flow, and changing the components or design of your shrine occasionally is very beneficial.

Remember that the world, like life, is solemn and playful at the same time, and both qualities are needed to remain balanced. Your shrine should embody both of these attributes. A crystal carved into a playful shape—a hippo or dolphin, for example—is an ideal addition.

Dendritic agate slice

Tumbled black onyx

Raw fire opal

Raw citrine

Pyrite 'sun'

Tumbled blue lace agate

CREATE A COSMIC HARMONY SHRINE

The following are suggestions. Use them as a starting point: your shrine is intimately personal to you, and you alone should decide what is placed there.

♦ First, decide what sort of base you wish to use. If the garden is your sanctuary, can you fence off a small area for your own use? A corner surrounded by your favorite scented shrubs, with a large flattish stone in the center or to one side, would be ideal. If the shrine is indoors, can you set up a permanent table or altar for your use? A small table with a drawer for the components and space for a cushion underneath is one idea. Alternatively, a thin flat rock, crystal, or piece of slate on which you can place your chosen items is easy to tidy away when not in use.

♦ Your heart crystal (see pages 74–75) should sit in the center of your shrine.

♦ You may wish to surround your heart crystal with crystals representing the elements. These can be from any tradition. In the Eastern tradition, fire is represented by red crystals; metal is represented by grey, white, or silver crystals; water is represented by blue crystals; wood is represented by green crystals; and earth is represented by yellow crystals. In the Western tradition, fire is represented by red crystals; water is represented by blue crystals; earth is represented by black crystals; air is represented by yellow or purple crystals; and spirit is represented by transparent or white crystals.

♦ You might also like to add other items that appeal to you, such as a candle, incense, or a small bowl of water. You could include some labradorite or white opal to symbolize spirit. Tektites are meteoric glass (usually black or dark red in color, although moldavite is a beautiful green), and are ideal representations of space, symbolic of the outward and upward aspirations of the human spirit. A flint arrowhead suggests your distant past, while a tiny crystal sphere points to the future.

♦ The shrine represents you, your beliefs, and your dreams. Set your imagination free.

6 HALLWAY AND FAÇADE
Networking and
the environment

A home's hallway and façade are associated
with the element of metal and with the color
silver (ranging from transparent through
white to gray). In this chapter you will find out
how using crystals in these home spaces
helps to foster meetings with helpful people,
improve connections with your neighbors
and support change and travel.

CRYSTALS FOR THE HALL: **GATEWAY TO THE WORLD**

Coming home after a grueling day's work should be like walking into an embrace–welcome back!–but many hallways are actually gloomy, impersonal places. Even minor changes to this often neglected part of the home can lift your spirits when you step through the door, hastening your recovery from the stresses and strains of everyday life.

ENLIVENING HALL CRYSTALS

Here are a few suggestions to give your hallway a more positive, invigorating feel.

- A sparkling crystal mobile hanging in the hallway offers a cheery reception and, by reflecting light from the open front door into all the rooms that open off the hallway, refreshes the chi of the whole house. Combining this cluster with a wind chime greatly enhances the effect: choose the chimes to complement your decor–wooden chimes add a mellow yin tone, while tinkling metal gives an invigorating yang note.

- A hanging crystal cluster is particularly recommended where stairs descend directly toward the front door. Positioned between the lowest step and the door, the crystals help to slow the chi that might otherwise cascade down and rush straight out the house, emptying the upper story of its atmosphere. The crystal facets also help to direct incoming chi up the stairs, allowing its energizing influence to circulate more easily around the higher level.

- Three crystal features placed along a long, narrow hallway will partition it into smaller sections. Ideas include large natural specimens, carved ornaments, and gem trees (see pages 62–63), as well as the usual hanging cascades.

- Light-colored shiny crystals arranged on tables or shelving, or even hung on the walls themselves, can significantly lift the ambience of a poorly lit hallway, particularly if they are reflected in a mirror on the facing wall.

- A bright crystal feature located in the corner where a hallway turns at a right angle can prevent the facing wall seeming like a dead end, and will help chi to flow around and along the hallway.

- A harmonizing crystal, such as clear quartz, is traditionally hung between doors that face each other directly across a narrow hallway, particularly if one door leads to the bathroom.

Amethyst cluster

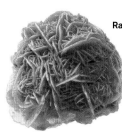

Raw selenite desert rose

Tumbled hematite

The sparkling brilliance of a faceted crystal brightens a dark hallway, and encourages the circulation of healthy chi throughout the home.

CRYSTALS FOR THE FRONT DOOR

The front door is probably the most important door in the home, and its primary function is to provide security from intruders.

- Specular hematite is famed as the most effective mineral for reflecting negative influences, so placing a polished specimen within sight of the door is a popular remedy for warding off chi generated by a hostile environment. The ideal shape for this guardian crystal is a large obelisk or pyramid, but even a rounded one is effective. Although this sentinel stone helps to counteract chronic feelings of vulnerability, glimpsing it should also remind you to be cautious when answering the door to strangers.

- The two halves of a rock-crystal geode (originally a cavity lined with crystals) positioned on either side of the specular hematite will balance the protective influence of the sentry and offer welcoming hospitality to friends. The combination of these dark and light crystals also impart a stabilizing influence, which helps to center and strengthen you, as you prepare to cross the threshold and pass from the safety of your home into the world at large.

Citrine geode

Apophyllite cluster

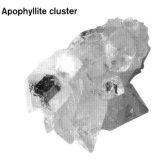

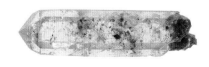

Quartz point

MENTORS AND **HELPFUL PEOPLE**

You cannot exist without other people. No matter how much of a loner you consider yourself to be, you rely on others in order to live.

Think for a moment of the number of individuals who make your life possible. Who built your home? Who provides the heat, power, and water? Who made the furniture? Who supplies your food? Who pays you for your work? Who cares for you when you are ill? And who works underground or unseen to keep your environment clean and healthy? The answers to some of these questions may of course be "me," but for most people, others perform these services.

Who is more important: the CEO making money for shareholders, the teacher instructing the citizens of tomorrow, or the sanitation engineer preventing the spread of deadly diseases? Everyone serves others, in one way or another, even if only as a consumer buying the fruits of other people's labor. This is another way in which everyone is interrelated.

Naturally, some people (outside your own family) are more personally important to you than others: a teacher, trainer, or patron perhaps, or even someone famous who affects your life. Those who have encouraged you to make the most of your abilities, who have taught you who and what you are, and who have equipped you to thrive in your chosen lifestyle are your mentors, role models, and heroes. You respect them and look up to them, and often model yourself on them.

TAKE INSPIRATION FROM A MENTOR

Take a few minutes to consider why your mentors mean so much to you. Is it because of their knowledge? Their charisma? Their behavior? Have you ever met them, or is your admiration based solely on what you know of them (for example, if they are a historical figure)?

♦ Find a carved crystal figure that symbolizes your mentor. It's fairly easy to find figurines of Buddha or Kuan Yin (the Chinese goddess of compassion and healing); or, if you wish, choose a deity from your own faith or tradition. Alternatively, select an animal that best represents your mentor: an elephant, perhaps, for wisdom and advice; a tiger for strength and stamina; a dragon for protection; or a swan for grace and artistry.

Raw labradorite

♦ Ideally the figure should be carved from rock crystal—or, if you can find it, labradorite or spectrolite. Both these crystals look gray until they are turned in the light, when a deep rainbow of color appears—ideal for reminding you to view those around you in a different light, no matter how dull they may at first appear. (If you're unable to find a carved stone, buy a small piece of crystal and place it near your chosen figure.)

♦ Position the figurine where you can see it on entering and leaving your home, beside the door in the hall, if possible. Let it inspire you throughout the day.

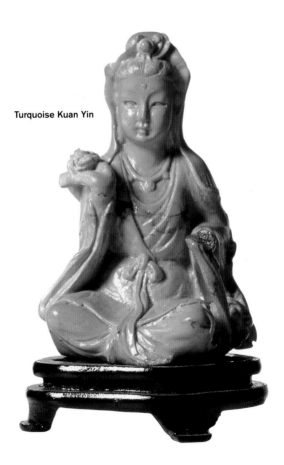

Turquoise Kuan Yin

Jade Buddha

AN OPEN **MIND**

The hall is the interface between your home and the outside world. From the hallway you step away from the familiar into the new—new places, new experiences, and new encounters.

The worst thing you can do with your mind is imprison it. Yes, of course you need your own beliefs, principles, and ethics—but to refuse to listen to and consider anyone else's opinions is an abuse of the greatest resource you will ever possess. Tolerance, receptivity, curiosity: these are the source of your greatest achievements. They lead to vision, inspiration, and the determination to learn, to better yourself and those around you. They allow you to pass beyond the façade and perceive the reality behind surface appearances.

There's an old adage that says, "You can't teach an old dog new tricks." It's complete nonsense: if the will is there, anyone can learn at any age, though the older you grow, the longer it may take, and since everyone has different aptitudes and abilities there are some things you may never be able to do. In such instances it's perhaps better to work with what you know you can accomplish, in a familiar field—which does not preclude the possibility of making major changes in your outlook. This takes a conscious decision, however, and some degree of effort. You need to break old habits in the way you think and be willing to experiment with new ideas.

To break free of inbuilt habits, you first need to realize what they are. Do you dismiss an idea because you've always done so, without considering it? Do you repeat the views and opinions of other people, rather than taking the time to develop your own? Do you "go with the flow" of popular conceptions because you're too afraid—or too lazy—to speak out for what you really believe?

Get into the new habit of pausing for thought before you express an opinion or answer a general question. Were you going to speak your own mind or expound someone else's views? Have you considered the tone of voice you might use? Can you safely be honest in this situation? Sometimes the brutal truth is necessary, but often a measure of diplomacy is required.

Dull and inconspicuous on the outside, geodes have extraordinary inner beauty, but they must be opened—sometimes forcefully—before it can be seen.

TRY SOMETHING NEW

Decide to bring a new experience into your life, for the sheer enjoyment of novelty and breaking old habits.

♦ Your choice will to some extent depend on your personal circumstances, the time that is available to you, and your budget. It should, however, be something completely novel: a craft or activity you've always wanted to try, but never quite managed; or, for a greater challenge, something you don't really like the idea of and have never considered before (for more information and ideas, see Chapter 8 on The Study).

♦ Change can be frightening—but without it, you stagnate. Like stale air or chi trapped in an airtight room, refusing to make changes can have deleterious effects on your mental health. Even small changes are enough to keep you healthy. An open mind is like an open door, letting in the fresh air of new ideas and providing a means of escape from the old.

♦ To help you in this challenge, carry a small piece of tourmalinated quartz: the contrast of the black tourmaline embedded in the transparent quartz exemplifies how easily nature accommodates opposites. Contemplating this crystal may trigger ideas for ways in which you can do the same in your life.

Tumbled tourmalinated quartz

A SENSE OF **COMMUNITY**

Just as the hallway symbolizes the interface between your refuge and the larger world, so it also represents the boundary between you as an individual and you as a member of the wider community.

For many centuries the local community was the mainstay of life for ordinary people, providing refuge, a means of survival, and assistance to those who needed it. Neighbors often helped each other and were helped in turn, for the good of the whole. Neighborhood problems were mostly dealt with by the community that they affected.

Over time the structure of society changed. Life became more complex; communities fragmented as people moved from a primarily rural lifestyle into cities

USE CRYSTALS TO FOSTER YOUR COMMUNITY SPIRIT

You can enhance your own sense of belonging to the local community in the following ways.

♦ To encourage community spirit, place a large rock-crystal cluster on a shelf or windowsill in your hallway. Look for a cluster with a lot of points, preferably of different sizes (if you find one with other crystals scattered among the quartz points, even better). The points represent the individuals that make up your neighborhood, set on a solid base, and act to remind you that you are a part of that community.

♦ Carry a Chinese writing stone with you—made of black limestone with white andalusite crystals that resemble Chinese characters—to help inspire you with ideas for fitting into your neighborhood, and with ways to change an existing pattern for the better.

Polished Chinese writing stone

full of strangers; occupations became both more complicated and less flexible. Stress became a major component of many people's lives. Power made its way into the hands of central "governments," which then decreed how everyone should act. Loneliness and alienation affected more and more of the population. Life became less secure and stable.

It's not possible to return to the "old days"—and most people wouldn't want to—but you can regain a sense of community spirit, even if you're not lucky enough to live in a neighborhood where it already exists. Being part of a community requires tolerance and compromise. Consider what qualities make a good neighbor—and whether you are one yourself. Do you "fit in" with your neighborhood? Do you respect the needs and feelings of those around you? The family next door with its young

Strong, sustainable growth requires a strong, stable foundation, whether for a crystal cluster or a community.

children won't appreciate loud, night-long parties every weekend. Do your neighbors respect your own needs and feelings? Finding your garden or hallway full of other people's rubbish is not a pleasant way to start or end the day, and can cause a lot of upset.

Such problems are often caused by simple thoughtlessness, and in many cases a polite request to stop doing whatever is causing offense will be enough—the vast majority of people respond positively to courtesy. (In cases where this isn't sufficient to resolve the problem, it's usually best to let the appropriate authorities deal with it: vendettas can quickly spiral out of control.)

When you meet your neighbors, try smiling and saying hello in passing, if you don't already do so. It costs nothing and may start a mutually beneficial friendship. If there's a local neighborhood security scheme, try becoming involved, even if only peripherally: it's reassuring to know that others are looking out for you and your property, and joining such a local organization is a way of reempowering yourself to a small degree.

HOMECOMING

Coming home is a special part of the day, and investing a little time and energy into improving the appearance of your home—as seen from outside— can bring lasting rewards.

For ease of construction, most houses are designed using squares and rectangles, as are their building blocks (such as brick, stone, and concrete beams). This inherently angular appearance is often crowned by a pitched roof, like an upward-pointing triangle—the classic shape of fiery yang. If the walls or roof are made of fired clay (red brick and tiles are prime examples), then the preponderance of yang in the building's façade can be overwhelming and may need to be balanced by some yin features.

WAYS TO COUNTERBALANCE YANG

- One popular method of counterbalancing a building's yang energy is to install a water feature (water being a yin element), such as a small pond in the front garden. There is a wide range of pond designs, but an informal one is undoubtedly best here. Plant it with low-growing flowers (blues and yellows, perhaps) set in a small rockery of rounded stones.

- A neat alternative to a garden pond is a circle of smooth pebbles arranged not in a heap, but in concave form, like a nest. You can easily do this on a level surface by positioning the largest pebbles in a ring and infilling the space with progressively smaller stones toward the middle. Avoid igneous rocks such as granite, because these are symbolically yang; instead, choose sedimentary rocks such as limestone or shale, which are formed under water and help to enhance the yin component. Sandstones may also be used; but don't use red sandstone, which forms in a desert (yang) environment.

WAYS TO REFLECT EXCESS CHI

Many homes in an urban environment are dominated by the surrounding buildings, which jostle too closely for comfort or simply rise so high that you are living in their shadow. Even street furniture (such as a lamppost or telegraph pole directly outside) can have a subtle but powerful effect on the way you feel about your home. Traffic driving directly towards a house situated at the end of a dead end, or facing a T-junction, generates chi that can rush headlong into the home and cause all

Tumbled smoky quartz

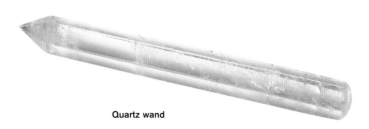

Quartz wand

A water feature near the entrance to your home balances too much yang energy and encourages the flow of healthy chi into the building.

manner of upset. The path to the front door may have a similar (though less acute) effect and, wherever possible, should be curved rather than straight. Fortunately, tradition offers straightforward solutions to these and other factors that intrude on the tranquility and privacy of your home.

- A shiny object positioned above, beside, or even on the door can reflect away some of the excess chi. It might be simply a quartz wand or faceted glass sphere, or a crystal cascade hung over the door.
- For the artistically minded, a mosaic plaque showing the house number or name in dark stones (such as smoky quartz) surrounded by lighter shiny crystals (such as milky quartz) is ideal, as long as it is clear from a distance, both by day and by night.
- Keeping a metal doorknob or mail box polished is another effective way to reflect an over-abundance of chi, but the most commonly used cure derived from the Chinese art of placement is a small circular mirror (specular hematite could be used instead), framed with a border showing the Early Heaven *ba gua* (see pages 78–79). This not only reflects negative chi, but also acts to harmonize the energies that do enter the home.

Tumbled specular hematite

Rose quartz wand

THE JOURNEY OF **LIFE**

Your front door, linking the façade of your building and the hallway, is your portal to the world. Inside is your own space, your home; outside is a place full of fascination and potential danger.

There are few places on the planet that can't now be reached by the intrepid traveler: whether you opt for a day trip to a nearby historical site, two weeks of sunbathing on the beach, a round-the-world cruise, or a month's trekking in the mountains depends on your health, budget, and spirit of adventure.

Mental voyages, from within the privacy of your own mind, can take you even further—and cost considerably less. Without the right attitude, however, any travel (physical, mental, or virtual) will be a waste of time.

Ask yourself if you feel comfortable at home, within yourself? Or do you use travel as a means to escape your duties, responsibilities, and the things about yourself that you don't like? There's no harm in getting away for a while, and a change of scene and pace often helps to give you a clearer perspective – but your problems will probably still be there when you return. Unless you're traveling specifically to give yourself breathing space, it's better to resolve whatever difficulties you can before leaving, especially if they lie within yourself. That way you can make the most of your travel opportunities.

If you feel at home with yourself, your own chi is balanced and free-flowing (and vice versa). You view life from a strong, self-assured base, secure within yourself and confident of your ability to cope with the unexpected. Life is perhaps best seen as a journey, and you need to make sure you're properly equipped for the trip. If you're confident you have all you need, you'll be better able to enjoy the journey.

CRYSTALS FOR TRAVEL

Whether your journey is internal or external, mental or physical, you don't want to be laden down with too much baggage— and this is as true of crystals as it is of emotional hang-ups, grudges, or suitcases. Small, inexpensive crystals are both more easily carried and less likely to attract attention.

♦ Before your journey, choose one crystal to represent yourself. Most people have a favorite crystal, perhaps a "birthstone" in a ring or on a pendant. Wear or carry it for good fortune.

♦ Try carrying a small, smooth piece of specular hematite for talismanic protection against ill will, but make sure you take physical precautions as well.

♦ Alternatively, stilbite (in the form of a bowtie or wheatsheaf) is the ideal talisman for any travel. It suggests a wide range of factors combining into a single movement, toward a future full of possibilities.

♦ If your journey is inward, choose a crystal that symbolizes the mystery within you: opal, perhaps, or blue sunstone.

♦ If your journey is back to the place of your birth, take citrine for communication, or moss agate to foster family feeling.

♦ If you are taking a vacation in an unfamiliar place, select a crystal that represents that place: for example, a blue crystal for the sea; green for forest; white for a winter vacation; patterned agate for a cultural tour. Use your imagination— and enjoy the experience.

Raw stilbite

Raw citrine

Tumbled specular hematite

Tumbled moss agate

Traveling should be a pleasure, something exciting and educational as well as entertaining. Enjoy the anticipation as well as the trip.

7 CHILDREN'S ROOMS
Creativity and new beginnings

Children's rooms (like the home's hallway and façade) are associated with the element of metal and with the color silver, ranging from transparent to white to gray. These rooms represent the inventive spark and a fresh start in life. In this chapter you will learn how to use crystals in these spaces to help develop creativity and plan for the future.

CRYSTALS FOR THE PLAYROOM:
BUILDING A BRIGHTER WORLD

There is, perhaps, nothing quite as receptive as a child's mind. Even in the womb, a baby's brain is building up ideas about the world, listening to the sounds of its parents' voices, for example, and growing accustomed to the routines of daily life. Once the child is born, that passive awareness quickly extends into an insatiable thirst for activity and discovery.

Time spent together with your child, enjoying the beauties of the natural Earth, can be quality time of the highest order and should be cherished. The single most important factor for children's rooms is safety, so take precautions when introducing a child to crystals. Powdery and sharp specimens, for instance, should never be given to young children, and care should always be taken with rounded crystals that might resemble candy and constitute a choking hazard. Supervision is recommended until you are confident that a child is sufficiently responsible to avoid risks.

STIMULATING PLAYROOM CRYSTALS

In keeping with the brightness of a child's mind, shiny crystals are best for the playroom, and transparent, translucent, sparkling, white, or silvery stones are ideal.

- The quartz wand is a firm favorite, but note that quartz tends to be brittle, so don't let a youngster use it as a hammer. Quartz glow stones, on the other hand, are perfect for hard knocks, as the resulting internal flashes of electricity are a source of entertainment.
- Try to introduce as wide a variety of forms, shapes, and sizes as you can. Large natural specimens are best, particularly those that show faceted crystals growing on their natural matrix.
- The double refraction of optical calcite is a challenge to inquiring minds of any age. (And tips taken from Chapter 8, on the study, can also be applied to the playroom if your child has a desk or other special space here that is used for homework.)

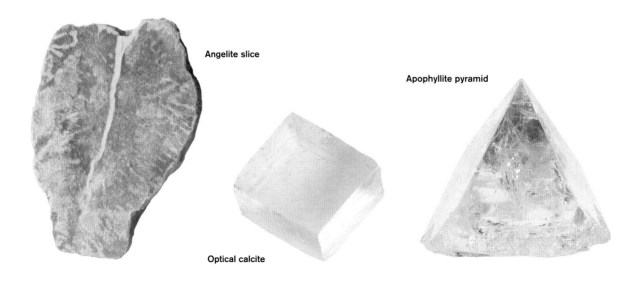

Angelite slice

Apophyllite pyramid

Optical calcite

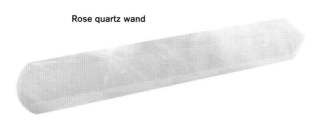

Rose quartz wand

Apophyllite cluster

• A crystal wind chime that resonates in the breeze from an open window makes a wonderful addition to a child's playroom. When the crystals catch the sunlight, they can also scatter beautiful and energizing mini-rainbows around the room.

Having beautiful crystals on permanent display in a child's playroom creates a lovely environment for children to develop in. However, growing minds tend to exhaust their interest in an object surprisingly quickly, so you should introduce new specimens regularly. Do keep the old ones, though, because within weeks or months the child will have made a quantum leap in development and will be ready to explore the old crystals with renewed interest and enthusiasm.

It is important, however, both for your own peace of mind and for the long-term development of children, that clutter in the playroom should be kept to a minimum. This means clearing toys and unused crystals away into

colorful and spacious storage spaces at the end of each day, ready to start afresh the next morning.

Sea shells are other traditional symbols of learning, and the spiral form of the conch is a valuable teaching aid, revealing how life's cycle of ups and downs is no mere rotation, but actually propels one through a third dimension. The process of learning continues throughout life, as a child's (and then an adult's) healthy curiosity seeks to explore and comprehend the infinite complexity, yet breathtaking simplicity of the world.

Amethyst geode

Tumbled rutilated quartz

Cubic iron pyrite

CRYSTALS FOR A CHILD'S BEDROOM:
RESTFUL AND SAFE

Children's surroundings are vital to their healthy development, and you should strive to make them as stimulating as possible. It would be a mistake, however, to cram a bedroom with bright toys and noisy activities—everyone needs the chance to relax, and children especially require plenty of rest. You need to provide a balance between activity and leisure, yang and yin.

The young brain soaks up everything it can, and although it cannot understand much of what it learns, it instinctively tries to make sense of it all. One vital tool that everyone uses throughout life to help piece together the contradictory elements of life is dreaming. Sleeping in a bedroom that makes them feel content, safe, and secure makes a huge difference to the sort of dreams children experience.

Children automatically mold themselves to their surroundings, which is actually the key to humans' success as a species, because each new generation adapts itself to fit its environment—and, of course, nature favors the fittest.

REASSURING BEDROOM CRYSTALS

If you have a choice of rooms for children, try to give them a bedroom that enjoys a view that faces the sunrise, which will allow them to benefit from invigorating morning chi. The crystals suggested below are ideal for relaxing a child, yet strengthening the imagination, and can help stimulate potent and creative dreams.

- Handling smooth crystals at bedtime is an ideal way for children to relax and let the day's tensions begin to drain away, but make sure they do not represent a choking hazard. Some polished clear quartz crystals display internal flaws that generate a spectrum of iridescent colors. Holding these (egg or ball shapes are ideal) so that they catch the light from a bedside lamp is a thoroughly soothing pastime.

- Small geodes with drusy (granular) clear quartz crystals are fun for young children, who delight in putting the halves together like a jigsaw; they then peek inside as they open them up again, watching the little jewels sparkle in the light. Closing the geodes to

Tumbled rose quartz

Quartz crystal ball

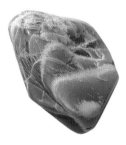

Tumbled moonstone

make it "sleepy-dark" inside can be a useful precursor to settling a child down to sleep. Sometimes, though, children prefer to leave the halves open, allowing their imaginations to continue wandering among the tiny crystals as they drop off to sleep.

- The rainbow hues of white opal are a real delight for a dozy child, who enjoys the gentle play of light inside the crystal.
- The chatoyancy—or twinkling, reflective nature—of a good moonstone is another soothing visual wonder.
- Rutilated quartz and "phantom" quartz crystals (see pages 138–139) are fascinating stones for pondering the mysteries that lie beyond surface appearances.
- Children can also benefit from the tips given earlier (see pages 32–33) regarding what can be seen on sitting up in bed (replace the pink crystals with white ones). If a child cannot easily see the door from his bed, position a reflective crystal such as an agate slice in the corner of the room, to provide a reassuring glimpse of the entrance.

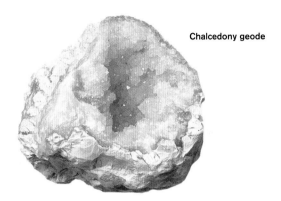

Chalcedony geode

Double-terminated phantom quartz

Citrine geode

Clear quartz with rainbow

Quartz polished egg

BOOST YOUR **CREATIVITY**

There is a child inside everyone. Depending on what you do and how you have developed, it may be deeply hidden, but it's there nevertheless: the source of your creativity as well as your sense of wonder. The problem is that in adult life, with all its stresses and problems, people often ignore or completely lose touch with the child within.

This may be because you have been pressurized into believing that, as an adult, childlike activities and thoughts are inappropriate–things you should have outgrown. But why? To children, everything is an adventure and all things are possible. To lose that openness and spontaneity is wasteful and unnecessary.

It's possible to regain some of those qualities, although relearning how to "play" may take some time and effort. Some people find the whole idea embarrassing; others may be unable to see any benefit in reverting to an earlier stage of life; other people may dismiss it as a waste of time. Yet without it, you are missing a considerable slice of your heritage.

Take some time out to watch children–young children, six years and below–at play. They use all their senses, enjoying and experiencing the world with their whole bodies, unselfconsciously and wholeheartedly, learning while they play. You need to emulate that outlook in order to retrieve the openness you once knew and discover fresh insights.

The creative mind responds instinctively to surroundings that inspire the mind. Decorate creatively and keep your imagination bright.

LEARN HOW TO PLAY

One of the easiest ways to accomplish this is with your crystals, because this can be done in private, thus avoiding any embarrassment you might feel.

♦ In the children's room–or the space in your home that approximates to it, your own "playroom"–sit for a while with your chosen crystals (any that appeal to you, but preferably a mix of colors, shapes, and sizes).

♦ Close your eyes and handle them, and see if you can tell them apart by touch.

♦ Roll your chosen crystals in your hands: do they evoke any particular feelings?

♦ Look at each of the crystals individually. Very often patterned stones (such as jasper, malachite, and lace agate) seem to have shapes within them: faces, animals, plants. Transparent crystals (rock quartz, amethyst, and citrine) often have "flaws" within them, which create

beautiful rainbow sprays when turned in the light. What can you see in your crystals? Do they form any recognizable shapes or patterns?

♦ Play with your crystals. Give them names, make up stories about them, see if they will talk to you.

♦ This exercise is best done in natural light, though you can try it in artificial light as well, to see the different effects it creates. Play music if you like.

♦ Engage all your senses: burn some incense, or open a bottle of your favorite fragrance (don't restrict yourself to perfume; if you like the smell of coffee, other strong-smelling foods, or even mustard, use that instead).

♦ Have a drink to hand: try something you've never drunk before, such as iced coffee or sparkling elderflower and apple juice; or maybe something you drank as a child.

♦ Vary the exercise's elements each time you try it. Most importantly, have fun!

Tumbled moss agate

Dendritic agate slice

Raw chrysanthemum stone

Raw fire agate

Chiastolite slice

Angelite slice

THE WONDER OF **THE NEW**

No matter how many opportunities there are for trying new activities, foods, or forms of entertainment, it's surprisingly easy to get stuck in a rut, repeating the same things over and over again. Sometimes this is due to anxiety—it's much more comforting to stay with the old and familiar, for the new and strange can be alarming; or to lethargy—it's far less bother to stick with the old; or to lack of time. However, by standing still you deprive yourself of a great deal of pleasure, stimulation, and the potential to change your life; you restrict yourself to one room, instead of using it as the base from which to go out and explore.

Children don't have this problem. To a child, everything is new and exciting. They haven't yet learned what is and isn't possible, and their minds are open to everything that life can make happen. You need to rediscover that ingenuousness, that fascination with life, in order to properly enjoy it.

Visiting new places, meeting new people, trying new things: all promote the generation of new ideas. Never be afraid to try something new. Apophyllite (a beautiful transparent crystal with extraordinary clarity and brilliance) is ideal as a talisman for fostering new ideas: it promotes lucidity and a practical framework for nurturing your child—whether this is your physical offspring or a brainchild. If possible, find crystals with plenty of internal flaws, as these will create patterns and

rainbows as the light plays over and through them. (In a child's room, place them out of reach where the sun can shine on or through them; the points, while not overly sharp, can still cause damage if not handled with care.)

Learning to appreciate the treasures that surround us is an important part of life. Our children are our greatest treasures—our contribution to the future.

QUESTION YOURSELF

Children never stop asking questions, and perhaps the most frequent one is "Why?" If you have young children of your own, take time to talk to them—and listen to what they say. If you don't have children, listen to other people's children, and imagine yourself as a child again, seeing the world as though for the first time.

♦ Speak to children on their own level. You aren't trying to teach or instruct them, or tell them what to do, in this exercise—quite the opposite: you are learning from them, listening to their view of the world you share, opening your mind and broadening your perceptions.

♦ Spend a couple of hours asking "Why?" concerning everything you think, say, or do. Your answers may surprise you.

Apophyllite cluster

♦ Then spend an hour or so asking "Why not?" If your answer is "Because it's a childish thing to do," ask yourself why that's such a bad thing.

♦ At the very least you'll get an insight into children's minds, and a new perspective on your own. If you're lucky, you may also find a new way of working, thinking, or making your life more productive or enjoyable (or both).

♦ Think of two everyday activities that you regard as chores, then think of the most unusual ways to perform them. It doesn't matter if what you come up with is completely impractical—the aim of the exercise is to think differently, creatively, and to broaden your perspective. Can you use elements of those new methods to change the chores into something more agreeable? This activity does not need to be confined to the playroom.

TREASURE HUNT

To a child, everything is a source of wonder, and the most common object can become a much-loved treasure. This is an outlook most people lose as they grow older, but rediscovering it enables you to value truly what you have.

Everyone is stardust! Forged in a stellar furnace and scattered through the cosmos by the explosive force of a supernova, this dust was captured in the gravity of the Earth's forming sun, and eventually formed the planet, its rocks and crystals, and human beings. So it makes sense to learn to appreciate the Earth's natural resources.

Learning to appreciate the treasures that surround us is an important part of life.

EXAMINE THE RESOURCES AROUND YOU

This exercise can help you in two ways: not only does it make you aware of natural resources that you probably take for granted, but it helps you to value the complex potential that lies all around you.

♦ Start small and easy, in the safety and familiarity of the playroom (or children's bedroom), and work outward: explore your home—with your children, if you have any; by yourself, if not. If you need an excuse, tell yourself that you're spring-cleaning: a home uncluttered by junk is one in which chi can flow more readily, so you are performing a valuable service for yourself.

♦ Every home is full of crystalline minerals, though at first you might not recognize them. Brick walls, rubble foundations, tile roof, glass windows, metal nails and screws, copper wiring and piping, the optical glass fiber in tele-communications, rock-wool and glass-fiber insulation, water in pipes, ice in the freezer, metal saucepans, clay crockery, glasses, metal cutlery, electronics components, plastics (made from mineral oil) of all varieties. The list is endless.

♦ Count and list the different types of metals in your home. Your list might easily include iron or steel, copper, aluminum and lead (and don't forget the rarer metals contained in some batteries). Hopefully you'll manage to find some gold—precious and incorruptible—to include in your list.

♦ As well as discovering all the minerals around you, consider those that lie inside you: from the iron in your blood and the calcium in your bones to the salt in your tears. Sit for a while and contemplate your own intricacy.

USEFUL CRYSTALS

• A bloodstone, with its spots of ruddy-colored iron, is an ideal crystal to carry around while you're hunting for the different metals in your home.

• Selenite's cool white beauty is excellent as a focus for meditation. Named for the moon goddess Selene, this crystal symbolizes both change and predictability, the steady, regular phases of the moon and this satellite's effect on the Earth.

• Optical calcite is a fascinating crystal, presenting a double image when you look through it. As a talisman, this transparent crystal presents you with two different views of the same thing. Contemplating this can help you perceive the ordinary as wonderful—and vice versa, because even the most wondrous thing is rooted in day-to-day reality.

Tumbled bloodstone

Selenite pillar

Optical calcite

THE GENERATIONS

Life is an ongoing process: an obvious statement, but one that is sometimes forgotten in the never-ending business of making a living. Most traditions place considerable emphasis on the responsibility of the family to care for its own members, especially those who are unable to care for themselves—in other words, the young and the old.

Few things excel the joy surrounding the birth of a new life, and rightly so. The boundless potential, the possibilities and hopes: children are the future and deserve the very best you can provide for them, so that they may be secure, healthy, and able to take advantage of all the opportunities that come their way. Your parents represent your past, your roots, and equally deserve respect and consideration, although such qualities should always be mutual.

Patience, tolerance, and compassion are essential elements in a healthy, happy family; they're also often the most difficult qualities to develop. Compromise is always necessary. So is communication, and a degree of tact. It's easy to assume you know best what those in your care require (and in the case of the very young, that's often the case), but it's also easy to forget that they are individuals in their own right and may have different ideas concerning their own needs. It's vitally important to take the time to listen to them, and then to put into practice what you learn.

CRYSTALS TO PROMOTE GENERATIONAL UNDERSTANDING

Milky quartz is a maternal, nurturing crystal. It has a long-standing reputation as a healing crystal, promoting steady recuperation from the minor illnesses to which

Sharing the moment and bridging the generations: the love of the family is timeless and selfless, grounding our lives and bestowing continuity upon them.

children—and the elderly—are prone. It has also traditionally been worn to help lactating mothers produce milk for their children. A large, egg-shaped milky quartz is an ideal crystal to hold when talking and listening to both young and old: its cool, smooth solidity acts as a reminder to remain calm and give others the time to express themselves. It's a comforting crystal, too, for youngsters to handle when they are out of sorts (as long as it's too large to fit in the mouth), making it a perfect addition to children's rooms.

Another excellent crystal is white marble, and a small piece should be positioned on the windowsill of a child or elder's room. Traditionally a protective crystal, it is ideal for use as a talisman for anyone who is under emotional stress. This is often the case when dealing with the elderly, because there is no escaping the fact that the end of life is death—not something that anyone likes to think about. Yet a peaceful end, after a life well lived, full of love and compassion, is nothing to fear. While there is life, however, a small, smooth piece of this crystal can remind you to make the most of each moment, regardless of the momentary frustrations and irritations that may occur. Never forget that life is a precious thing, much to be treasured.

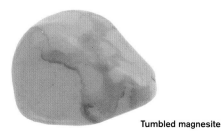

Tumbled magnesite

8 THE STUDY
Education and lifelong learning

This room of the home is associated with the element of earth and with the colors yellow, blue-green, and turquoise. The study represents the desire for education and the longing to find out more about yourself. In this chapter you will discover how crystal talismans here can inspire you to acquire knowledge and explore your inner potential.

CRYSTALS FOR THE STUDY:
GETTING THE BRAIN IN GEAR

With all the competing distractions of today's relentless consumer culture, it can be really difficult to muster the self-discipline to settle down alone and study, undisturbed. Fortunately, crystals can have a powerfully calming effect on us, and their great age counteracts the lure of immediate gratification. Crystals can help you to make your study room a powerhouse of creativity and positive change.

RESTFUL CRYSTALS FOR THE STUDY

The right combination of crystals can not only steady the mind and put you in the mood to study, but can also stimulate you to study more effectively.

- The pale opacity of turquoise exercises a calming influence that promotes a good atmosphere for contemplation. The popularity of this semiprecious stone makes it readily available in a wide range of ornamental shapes, which are perfect for desktop use as paperweights. A turquoise egg held comfortably in the hand while you're reading, thinking, or studying for examinations can help to clear your mind of extraneous clutter; this shape of crystal is known as a "worry-egg," because kneading it is a well-known way to relieve tension (and can reduce exam nerves in particular).

- A citrine sphere or agate slice, or other reflective surface, positioned to provide some warning of other people's approach, is useful if the door to your study is not in your line of sight. As with the home office, this will help prevent you being constantly on edge about being disturbed.

- A string of amber or other yellow crystal beads draped over tiers of shelves, like tinsel over the boughs of a

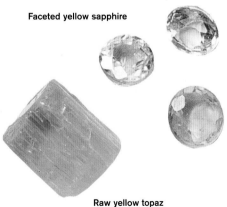

Faceted yellow sapphire

Raw yellow topaz

Polished turquoise

Polished amber

Christmas tree, softens the knife-blade effect of the shelves and the jutting spines of books. Shelves near seats are best draped with darker beads to make them less intrusive and intimidating. Place here books that are consulted less frequently—otherwise the chore of having to move the beads to reach your favorite books will soon become an irritation and create a mental block. Books that are never consulted can become areas of tired or even stagnant chi, so it is best to move them out of the main study area, or even let them go to someone else who could benefit from them more than you. Bookshelves should never be crammed: leave some gaps to allow chi to permeate with ease (however, some bindings can be damaged if books lean awkwardly, so use turquoise ornaments to fill the spaces).

• A silicon chip lies at the heart of every computer, calculator, and digital watch, and this silicon comes from a crystal grown in carefully controlled laboratory conditions. The true beauty of these chips, with their complex surface of microscopic circuitry, is not readily visible to the naked eye (and many are enveloped in a black protective casing). However, they can make attractive specimens when mounted, framed, and hung in the southeast of the study, where they encourage an alert relaxation that helps you to assimilate and process ideas more rapidly. They are also a powerful reminder that today's culture is not so very different from that of Stone Age society—whose flint tools, for example, are faceted gems of craftsmanship, the cutting edge technology of its time—and tomorrow's civilization will one day seem as primitive and crude.

Raw citrine

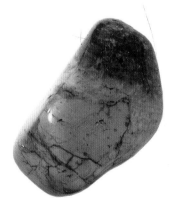

Tumbled yellow jasper

Faceted yellow tourmaline

WHAT TO **STUDY**

"Everyone needs a martial art and a musical instrument." This traditional oriental saying indicates that a balance between the academic, physical, and artistic is needed in order to be a fully rounded, well-educated person. For some people this is easy; for others it may be a struggle; but for everyone, making a list of personal strengths and weaknesses is the first step in deciding how to proceed.

Your academic days may be long over, but remember that learning is a lifelong thing—and essential if you wish to maintain any sort of control over your personal environment. In a culture where almost everything is controlled electronically, for instance, refusing even to consider learning the basics of using a computer is somewhat short-sighted. On the other hand, learning to windsurf at 80 years of age is probably beyond most people. It's important to preserve a sense of what is realistically possible.

If you have read Chapter 4 on the home office, you may already have made a list of your abilities and qualifications. If you haven't, make one now, then appraise it critically. In which areas are you lacking? Have you focused on scientific, artistic, or physical pursuits to the exclusion of everything else? If you work in information technology, is that all you do, even at home? Is there anything you've always really wanted to learn, but never quite managed to, because it wasn't useful in your job or life as a whole?

When it comes to learning, you can build on what you already have, using your existing foundations, but perhaps adding a new "room" by taking a more specialized subject in your current area of expertise; or you can decide to achieve balance by studying your worst subject. The latter is the more balanced approach and the one we would recommend—but only in so far as it results in a feeling of accomplishment and satisfaction.

Tumbled malachite with azurite

Raw larimar

ENCOURAGE YOUR OWN METAMORPHOSIS

Whatever you decide, remember the ancient oriental saying quoted at the outset, and try to choose subjects that balance your current skills. You might not want to learn to play a musical instrument—but how about community singing or learning to dance? From ice-dance through jazz and tap, line-dancing and folk-dancing to ballroom-dancing and salsa, it's usually possible to find one style that appeals—and dance has the added benefit of being healthy exercise, without the hard work.

Malachite and azurite is an attractive mixture of minerals, which is actually a single substance in the process of gradual chemical transformation; as such, it can help you adopt a positive mental attitude towards your own metamorphosis into a more well-rounded individual. Keep a specimen in your study space.

There is an amazing number of resources for discovering where and what to study. Talk to friends, family, neighbors, workmates, and professionals. Visit the library; check out local evening classes, hobby clubs, and special interest groups. Try surfing the Internet. You can find just about everything, if you really want to.

Before making a decision about what to study, make sure you prepare thoroughly: it's only sensible to be as well-informed as possible.

LIFELONG **LEARNING**

The thought of studying a new subject may be daunting, especially if it's been some time since you've tried to learn anything at all, but there are ways to make the experience positive, challenging, and stimulating. Everyone is a student in the University of Life, and with the right mental attitude and a little determination you can succeed in your chosen field.

When you are faced with a new subject, or are brushing up on an old one, remember an important historical lesson: divide and conquer. It's a great deal easier to learn anything if the subject is broken up into bite-size pieces, and this also prevents fatigue. You learn far more effectively if you give yourself time to take breaks and review what you've learned so far—and this works as well with life as a whole as it does with subjects under review in your study space.

Tumbled chrysocolla

Tumbled malachite

Raw citrine

SCRUTINIZE YOURSELF

Have you allowed society to label you a "has-been" or a "no-hoper"? Do you feel past your "use by" date, or left behind?

♦ Take a long look at yourself: not the physical you, but the inner self. Focus on the positive, not the negative—on the things you can do, not those you can't.

♦ Say no when you mean it, and keep saying it until everyone else realizes that you do mean it. You'll gain respect: both self-respect and the respect of others. No one has the right to tell you who or what you should be, or to try and stop you fulfilling your potential. Resist being labeled or pigeon-holed—but don't be aggressive, for that causes far more problems than it ever solves.

♦ On a slightly more pragmatic level, write down what you intend to accomplish in your chosen course of study. Do you want a qualification at the end of it? A change of job? Are you studying for fun, or simply to improve your understanding of a favorite topic? Do you want to keep up with your children, or just keep up with what's happening in the world? This is your written declaration—keep it in your study space and check it every now and then, to remind yourself of your original intention and to establish how far you've come.

♦ Employ the crystal known as "tigeriron," a banded mix of tiger's eye, red jasper, and hematite, which represents the strongest elements of all three crystals: tiger's eye to promote a deeper understanding of inner resources and the ability to use them; red jasper for strength and perseverance; and hematite to deflect negative influences, minimize panic attacks and foster an open, tolerant mind. It is the ideal crystal for all aspects of learning. Look at or hold a small "worry-egg" occasionally, or wear a piece of tigeriron jewelry while you work in your study space.

TESTING TIMES

Tests and examinations are all about rising to meet a challenge at a particular point in space and time. They are a way for you to prove, to yourself and to the world at large, how much and how well you have learned your chosen subjects (which is why cheating is never a good idea, because you are simply cheating yourself).

Consider the three broad areas of learning and their fundamental philosophies. There are several ways of perceiving them, but for the purposes of this book we'll view them thus:

- The arts and humanities energize your imagination and your ability to empathize.
- The sciences teach you to question, explore, and develop a rational approach to problems.
- Physical pursuits—from learning to drive, through sports or dance, to playing a musical instrument—increase your hand–eye and body–mind coordination.

Between them, these areas of learning result in a balanced and well-formed individual, who is able to cope with both the good and bad in life.

On a more specific level, tests and exams can have a significant effect on your life. If you don't pass your driving test, it is illegal to drive. Gaining entrance to your chosen college or university may depend on your exam results. Your chosen career—or your chances for promotion—might demand certain qualifications. In the abstract, this makes sense. The ability to pass exams shows that you are dedicated and able to work hard, have been able to memorize the necessary material and can use it to solve problems "on the spot," and have the discipline to succeed under stressful conditions.

There's no substitute for self-discipline, but studying with a crystal can help to both calm and inspire, and will make learning a pleasure.

Tumbled rutilated quartz

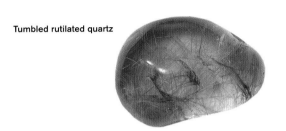

Tumbled tiger's eye

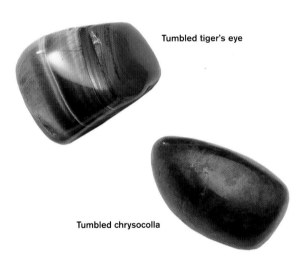

Tumbled chrysocolla

Double-terminated phantom quartz

A bad case of exam nerves can ruin a promising career, but you can take positive steps to defuse this crisis by developing a clear idea of Plan B: what to do if you fail. This will help you take the exam in your stride, and will mitigate both over-indulgence in the elation of success and panic in the wake of failure.

CRYSTALS FOR GOOD LUCK

No crystal can ever take the place of hard work, self-discipline, and study, but there are several crystals that can be used as talismans when you are sitting tests.

- Chrysocolla promotes and enhances artistic appreciation, and may also prove useful in art and music exams and interviews. Carry a small, tumbled piece as a "worry-stone" to relieve stress prior to the exam, and keep it in your pocket during the exam.
- Rutilated quartz enhances the swift transition from one idea to the next, and is useful in most tests.
- Tiger's eye symbolizes the integration of mind and body. If possible, wear a small piece during physical tests, perhaps as a ring or earring.
- A small, transparent rock crystal, in the shape of a wand with a natural point, is a crystal that anyone can carry with them as a personal talisman: it symbolizes clear, directed thought and intentions. Even better, if you can find one, is a natural double-terminated crystal (one with a point at both ends), which represents two-way communication and learning, and is ideal for use in the study.

OCCULT **KNOWLEDGE**

The word "occult" merely means hidden, and occultism is the study of things beyond the scope of day-to-day life. Occultists not only examine the great mysteries of life before birth and after death, but research practical matters, such as living in harmony with nature.

Careful observation over many millennia has uncovered a wealth of nature's hidden secrets, and modern science is continuing this work of revealing the detailed structure of the world.

CRYSTAL SYMMETRY

The internal structures of crystals were determined by X-rays early in the 20th century, revealing the symmetries that make them so different from ordinary rock. Three basic types of symmetry combine to produce seven conventional crystal groups, into which all crystals can be placed.

It is notable that the shapes of yin and yang are symmetrical: if you stuck a pin in the middle of the *tai chi tu* (see pages 10–11) and turned the symbol halfway around, the shapes would cover each other precisely. Two other sacred icons of the Chinese art of placement are also connected by symmetry: the Early Heaven *ba gua* and the *lo shu* (see pages 78–79 and pages 14–15 respectively).

The numbers on the *ba gua* are widely known, but there is another "hidden" tradition, in which the binary code (yang = 1, yin = 0) is read from the other direction. For the technically minded, 1 becomes 4 (and vice versa), and 3 becomes 6 (and vice versa), while the other numbers are unchanged. However, all you need to know is that a line drawn to follow this occult numerical sequence creates a pattern or sigil. Flip this sigil to its

The *ba gua* sigil

The mirror image of the *ba gua* sigil

The *lo shu* sigil

mirror image and rotate it one eighth of a turn, and it matches the *lo shu*'s own sigil precisely.

This key idea of changing of one thing into another simply by turning it symbolizes how even a small change can have significant consequences. A simple change of heart can turn despair into valor, making possible truly heroic feats.

Even moving a crystal slightly—perhaps just by rotating it to show a different side—can generate a completely new atmosphere in a room. Always feel free to experiment with your crystals, and indulge those periodic urges to rearrange things "just for a change." This is the only way to develop your own intuition and come to trust your instincts. Books can only take you so far—the rest of this unique journey is up to you alone.

THE FEAR OF KNOWLEDGE

Investigating secrets hidden in ancient lore is a fascinating study, but it is fraught with difficulties. Knowledge can confer power, and some people have a vested interest in keeping certain information secret. Like many kings, the ancient Chinese emperors claimed divine authority for their actions, and so before the Tyrant of Shang could be overthrown (in the 11th century BCE), the rebels had to free themselves from deep-rooted traditions of unquestioning allegiance.

One of occultism's most controversial purposes is to allow its students a trustworthy passage into full human maturity—a state of spiritual wakefulness that allows perfect freedom and independence of action. These enlightened individuals are often referred to as masters or sages, and have been relentlessly persecuted by authoritarian regimes throughout history.

A little knowledge can be a dangerous thing. Yellow jade, a form of jadeite (yellow calcite or tiger's eye may be used instead), is a useful worry-stone—keep it handy in the study for those moments when you need a sense of perspective amid life's deep and disturbing mysteries.

Gazing into a crystal sphere is unlikely to reveal the future, but as a focus for calming and settling the mind it is ideal.

CURIOSITY AND **INTEREST**

Learning should be fun, and so should studying—the two are not necessarily the same thing. Your ability to learn is made easier when your innate curiosity is aroused, rather than by memorizing dry facts and figures. You often learn best when you're free to follow an idea or a subject to its conclusion, whether or not that's what you're supposed to be doing (hence the popularity of surfing the Internet). It's amazing what you can learn in this way—and you certainly learn fastest when you discover something that feeds into or enlivens an existing interest.

Everything is connected. It's really not possible to study geography without taking into account the history, language, geology, or culture of the area in question. When studying literature, it helps to have a little knowledge of the writer, poet, or playwright and the culture in which he or she wrote, if you're to appreciate fully his or her work. And while pure mathematics has a beauty all its own, its greatest value is in its application to more practical matters.

We've already discussed the wisdom of balanced learning, in order to become a balanced person, but there's another element you should consider: studying a subject not because it will help your career, promotion prospects, or life in general, but purely for pleasure.

- Do you love orchids, but don't have the right conditions in which to grow them? Study them—find out everything you can about them, their names, their habitats, their folklore, and any medical properties they may possess.
- Do you live in an interesting location? Explore its history or its archaeology: check out your local museum for assistance.

From learning to play chess to growing orchids, from pottery to car repair, hobbies can be a source of pride, self-confidence, and even extra cash.

- Are you fond of a particular artist/make of car/regional cookery style? Learn all about them.

This kind of research stretches your mental muscle, exercises your thinking ability, and improves your memory in a completely stress-free way. It's study, but it's recreational rather than work.

STIMULATE YOUR OWN CURIOSITY

Use this exercise to arouse your own interest and to encourage yourself to learn more.

♦ To start off, choose two crystals—ideally one of them should be amber (see below)—and find out everything you can about them: where they came from; how they were collected; their natural shape; how they were formed and over what timescale; what gives them their color; whether they have any traditional talismanic or medicinal uses; and whether there's any folklore associated with them.

♦ Sort and prepare your researched material as though you were going to give a small informal presentation to a group of friends. This is an excellent way of learning to organize what you have discovered.

♦ Use amber to assist you: it's a fascinating fossilized resin from ancient pine forests, often with seeds or insects trapped within it. Amber is warm to the touch, very light in weight and its translucency resembles sunlight. It acts to promote creativity and spur the imagination, and you should wear or carry it for luck when taking part in quizzes, lateral thinking, or IQ tests.

♦ Keep a citrine crystal cluster in your study space to foster clarity of thought. But make sure it's kept clean and doesn't get dusty over time.

Amber jewelry

Polished amber

Citrine cluster

9 LIVING/DINING ROOM
Celebrity, status, and honor

The living or dining room is associated with the element of fire and with the color red. It symbolizes the way you perceive yourself, as well as your public image and reputation. In this chapter you will learn how the use of crystals in this space centers on your outward appearance and on your responsibilities to those around you.

CRYSTALS FOR **THE LIVING/DINING ROOM**

The living room tends to be the place where everything that doesn't belong anywhere else finds a home. It is the focus for family togetherness and, while it may be the scene of bouts of intense activity during the day, it must also accommodate evenings of pure relaxation. The dining room, likewise, is the venue for both noisy, boisterous family meals and intimate get-togethers for partners and lovers.

MULTIPURPOSE LIVING/DINING CRYSTALS

While a crystal chandelier showering bright rainbows over a festive occasion may not be appropriate for every living or dining room, there are plenty of ways in which crystals can add their special sparkle to these most important rooms.

- A simple faceted crystal ball hung over the center of the dining table helps to balance chi in this room, and may also act as an aid for embracing a healthier diet.
- Warm, red crystals are superb in the living room, as they simultaneously stimulate people to make good use of their time and remind them of the comforting glow of the fire—heart of the home. Red tiger's eye has chatoyant bands of light and dark that perfectly represent those alternate phases of action and stillness, making it an ideal and increasingly popular crystal for the living room. It can be used as a large specimen or as a carved ornament.
- A crystal wind chime (clear quartz is best) positioned in the window—if you are planning a daytime event, such as a community group meeting, where you need to generate plenty of energy and fresh ideas—will help spread chi into the whole room, stimulating enthusiasm. A faceted glass ball or shiny crystal mobile can work here too. Use these ideas at any time to maximize chi when a window is small or allows little light to enter.
- A large mobile of dark crystals (such as carnelian) hung in the window—if you're expecting a visit from someone whose natural exuberance tends to overwhelm—can calm the atmosphere and block some of the chi from entering, preventing your guest from

Tumbled amber

Red jasper polished egg

Vibrant red for yang energy, sparkling transparency for yin: such a cascade, hung to catch the light in the living room, is ideal for balancing chi.

dominating the whole rendezvous. Alternatively, small red amber beads may be sewn onto translucent curtains to reduce the amount of ambient energy in the room. Such techniques help people to relax and enjoy each other's company, promoting conversation, interaction, and the development of more profound relationships. And they may be used to counteract excessively large or bright windows.

- A bright crystal mobile hung from the ceiling can brighten a dark corner of the room.
- A bead curtain, with small red or clear crystals secured to each strand, can be used to screen off alcoves, especially on formal occasions. A voile curtain or other gauzy material may be used instead, but any crystals sewn to it should be very small to prevent them from deforming the cloth—red amber is light in weight, making it a popular option here. Do remember to take special care when washing fabrics adorned with crystals, as fine material can easily tear or the stones detach. Dry the fabric in the sunshine for the natural reenergizing of the crystals.

Raw carnelian

Tumbled red tiger's eye

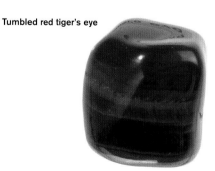

HOLDING **COURT**

The concept of hospitality is something that raises humans above the level of animals. To welcome someone into your home—whether that means your heart, your house, or your country—requires trust and a willingness to make yourself vulnerable. Sharing a meal has an even more profound significance: once someone has eaten in a host's home, that person is by tradition morally bound not to harm the host and his or her family (and vice versa).

Today it is less common than in the past for houses to have a separate dining room: the eating area is often part of the kitchen or living room and, generally speaking, when you invite people to your home, you show them into the living room. This is where they get their first firm impression of your home, and of yourself at home. You therefore want this room be comfortable and a reflection of your personality, and for the room to be relaxing for guests, you need to be relaxed yourself. That's easy enough with friends and close family, but with people you don't know so well it can be more problematic.

Making sure the room is clean and uncluttered is the best way to start; this not only creates a good impression and allows chi to flow freely throughout, but also means that you can concentrate on making your guests feel at home. It's traditional to offer food and drink of some kind, even if it's just coffee and cookies; if possible, use deep-red crockery on a dark-red or black tray. Ensure that whatever you're wearing is comfortable—after all, this is your home, and you don't have to dress up unless you want to.

The room usually has some sort of centerpiece, even if it's only the ubiquitous television set. Place a crystal where it will catch the light: warmly protective red tiger's eye carved into the shape of a bird is ideal and can look stunning placed directly under a spotlight. Red tiger's eye enjoys a reputation for building self-confidence and an appreciation of your own worth, helping any host or hostess to shine. If nothing else, suspend a red crystal—a small carved heart, perhaps—in the window to help circulate the room's chi.

Tumbled red tiger's eye

Tumbled red jasper

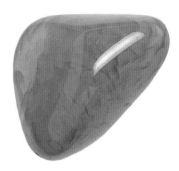

Tumbled carnelian

MAKE A CRYSTAL CENTREPIECE FOR YOUR TABLE

Try this exercise to create a unique, vibrant, and auspicious centerpiece for your dining table.

♦ Buy three rich red candles. Bear in mind that you will be cutting them to different heights, so very thick candles may be inappropriate, unless you have the right tools and your table is large; thin tapers will need to be secured in red or gold-colored holders.

♦ Leave one candle at its original height and place it on a large flat glass or stone base.

♦ Place the other two candles either side, forming a triangular shape, as shown. Trim the candles to make a ∧ shape (the Chinese art of placement's symbol for fire). Each candle should be a slightly different height, and the ∧ can be as tall and narrow or as broad and shallow as you wish.

♦ Soften the wax slightly and press small, smooth red jasper, carnelian, or red tiger's eye crystals into the candles.

♦ Scatter more stones around the base of the candles, and light them just before your guests enter the room.

PROMOTE **RELAXATION**

Promote Relaxation

The living room is a place of dynamic energy—lively rather than restful. Circulating yang chi makes it an excellent place for family and friends to get together, but can hinder relaxation. Being able to help guests unwind, even in an energetic environment, is a useful skill, a subtle balance of active and passive chi, and one that is well worth cultivating.

You need a flexible mental attitude and the ability to watch and listen—not only to what is being said, but to the undercurrents (what is being articulated in the facial expressions and body language of those around you). This takes a little practice, but once it is learned, you can feel relaxed and comfortable almost anywhere. And your own home is the best place to learn.

The perfect crystal talisman is a star ruby, with its famous asterism (starlike effect) created by three white lines combining in the center to form a six-rayed star. It symbolizes personal integration, self-knowledge combined with a rational but compassionate view of the world. However, star rubies are not common (much like the qualities they represent) and generally very expensive. A little easier to find are star rose quartz crystals, which make an ideal substitute. Never forget, though, that no matter how appealing the talisman, the ability to empower yourself comes from within.

It takes a lot of work to acquire a good reputation, but is distressingly easy to acquire a bad one. Yet the way you view yourself is, ultimately, far more important than the way others see you: self-respect is more precious than your reputation.

♦ Find or make a couple of hours when you can be alone and won't be interrupted.

♦ Make sure that your living room is tidy, so that chi can flow freely, and wear something comfortable. Keep distractions to a minimum, but play some music quietly and have incense or a fragrance burning if you choose.

♦ Sit comfortably and hold in your hand a spherical or egg-shaped red carnelian or red calcite (excellent for promoting emotional independence and fortitude).

♦ Relax and gaze at the crystal. Imagine yourself being the center of attention of a crowd of friends, and take note of your feelings. Do you enjoy being in this situation, or does it make you feel uneasy? Imagine yourself acting the part of hostess for them, behaving cheerfully but with quiet dignity. Play out an event—a dinner party, perhaps—in your mind, and see yourself behaving courteously, without being self-effacing. A trick to achieving this is to imagine your every action being watched or filmed by a hidden camera: not in a threatening way, but for use as a training guide for other people in the future.

♦ When you feel comfortable with this scenario, substitute strangers for your friends and mentally act out a similar occasion, again noting your reactions. Reenact the scene, making changes to your behavior as you see fit, until you're totally at ease with the situation. Then practice carrying that self-confident dignity with you and using it in your dealings with other people.

THE COURAGE OF YOUR **CONVICTIONS**

There comes a time when you must stop compromising and stand firm for your beliefs: not aggressively, but with determination. It takes a great deal of courage—particularly if what you believe in goes against popular opinion—but if you wish to be true to yourself, it is necessary. First, however, you need to feel strong and self-confident enough to face possible opposition or ridicule.

CRYSTALS FOR ASSERTIVENESS

It's easy to be aggressive toward other people, and possibly even easier to be submissive: fear often prompts one or other of these responses, although they rarely accomplish anything positive. Assertiveness without confrontation, firmness without capitulation, and the ability to compromise where necessary are far more effective courses of action. Each attempt to behave consciously in this way increases your ability, and each time it becomes easier.

Professional assertiveness training is beyond the scope of this book, but everyone can use the foregoing principles in daily life, and there is talismanic help available as well.

- Keep a fairly large piece of polished sardonyx, with its prominent red and black bands, in the living room, where you can see it whenever you look at your television, radio, phone, or computer: it represents both a shield and your fighting spirit, your response to the challenges that the world throws your way.

- Wear or carry a ruby (or its less expensive counterpart, the carnelian), which has a long tradition of use as a talisman promoting both courage and resilience in the face of hostility.

- A slightly more unusual talisman is a holey stone (a stone with a hole right through it). It symbolizes the willingness to be open, honest, and transparent: it is the yin at the heart of yang. Ideally you should find your own holey stone while out for a walk: perhaps at the beach, on a moor, or in a wood. It's often said that these stones find you rather than the other way around. Should this happen, regard it as a very special sign of positive, balanced chi infusing you, and place it in a prominent place in the living or dining room, where it may help to spread its influence throughout the entire house. A candle placed behind the stone may be lit to enhance its effect.

Faceted ruby

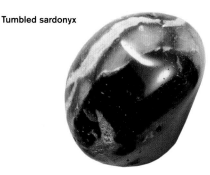

Tumbled sardonyx

Raw carnelian

EVALUATE YOUR ACHIEVEMENTS

Working through the exercises in this book will have given you a sense of self-worth, and an idea of your place in the world, but taking some time to consider what you have achieved is appropriate at this point.

♦ Make a list of your accomplishments. Include qualifications, bad habits you've broken, unsatisfactory behavior you've managed to change for the better, new insights you've learned—anything, in fact, that has made you more the person you want to be. Partial successes should also be included: they represent progress toward your goal.

♦ Next, consider the people whose lives you've affected in some way: parents, family, friends, teachers, employers, work colleagues—the list is, potentially, endless. Think for a moment of how different their lives would be if you weren't here, and of what they'd be missing.

♦ Realize that you matter. If you weren't here, there would be a you-shaped hole in the life of the world. Your beliefs and opinions are relevant, and you have every right to be heard—even if few people agree with you.

TAKE **RESPONSIBILITY**

The living room is just that—a room that represents the myriad elements that make up your life as a whole, as well as the room in which you spend a significant part of your personal life. It's a world in miniature—and being there should encourage you to consider the wider arena in which you exist.

There is only one habitable world, and while it's nice to think that one day humans might be able to live on other worlds, that isn't going to happen in the immediate future; and, even when it does, only the healthiest, most useful, and possibly wealthiest will be able to take advantage of the opportunity. It therefore makes sense to take care of the planet as it exists now—both for yourself and for those who come after you.

Everyone is responsible for their own thoughts, words, and actions. Upbringing and genetics play a part, of course, but ultimately *you* are accountable for yourself and for what you have accomplished—or not—in your life. Blaming someone or something else for your faults serves no purpose other than to make you look weak, foolish, and incompetent as a human being. Taking responsibility also means regaining power over your own life, making positive choices and defending your home, your family, your friends, and, most importantly, yourself.

Play your own small part in taking responsibility for your environment and the world around you.

♦ Start in small ways. When you need to replace an item in your home, opt for an environmentally beneficial, energy-efficient, fair-traded choice. Avoid using wood from rare and endangered trees. Choose natural fabrics where you can. Try to use fewer chemicals, especially those containing toxins. It may not seem like much, but every person who behaves responsibly places a little less stress on the planet. It makes you feel good about yourself, too.

♦ Apply the same precept when choosing crystals. Some countries have great riches in their rocks, but when financial pressures are applied, insufficient care may be taken to preserve the unique habitat of threatened species above the ground. The ideal talismanic crystal (a so-called "phantom" or "ghost" crystal) may prove a little difficult to find: these are natural quartz crystals that show their stages of growth, often as miniature replicas inside each other, rather like Russian dolls. They demonstrate not only that evolution usually finds a way to carry on after an apparent end is reached, but that humans live as just one part of a greater whole, which is difficult to grasp in its entirety from a limited human perspective. All crystals take millennia to grow: phantom crystals have their development interrupted at some point, then resume, sometimes in a different color. It's worth making an effort to find one of these treasures and giving it pride of place near the entrance to your living room, where it will remind you to consider your own place in the pattern of the world.

♦ Make a point, every time you leave the house, of doing one small thing to improve the place where you live. Switch off an appliance that you normally leave on and save energy; pick up a piece of garbage and dispose of it properly, recycling it if possible.

Double-terminated phantom quartz

Harmony between beauty and practicality, dynamic energy and restful tranquility, characterizes chi in balance—in your home as well as in yourself.

DRESSING **THE PART**

By now your home should have at least a couple of crystals that are both beautiful and useful, but hopefully not too many: discretion in choosing them is a sign of maturity. Your living room represents your "public face" within your home. Now it's time to consider crystals that you can carry with you when you leave this space: talismanic crystals that you can wear.

Jewelry is the most obvious, and perhaps the most attractive, way to wear crystals. Earrings, rings, bracelets, necklaces, traditional cufflinks or tie-pins, small beads for hair braids or piercings—there are countless options for personal adornment. Your own choice will depend on your intentions, or on elements of your personality in which you feel you are lacking.

- Blue or black jewelry: sapphire, turquoise, aquamarine, lapis lazuli, hematite, and onyx are the most common crystals. Wear them when you feel tense or stressed, or on occasions when you feel that your own

personality is being subsumed by another—that of your boss, for example.

- Pink or purple jewelry: garnet, rose quartz, and amethyst are most popular; sugilite and charoite less so, but still worth hunting down. Wear these crystals to assist in any aspect of relationships with friends, partners, and lovers.

- Green jewelry: emerald, peridot, malachite, and jade are best known. Wear them when dealing with family or domestic matters.

- Red and green jewelry: bloodstone and unakite are the most common; banded fluorite is less common, but is a good talisman for strengthening business communications. Wear these crystals when handling financial and business matters.

- Silver, white, and gray jewelry: plain silver, moonstone, spectrolite, and labradorite are the crystals most easily found. Wear them when dealing with community and

Individual choice in jewelry is an intimate and intensely personal matter. Take the time to choose with care: let your choice reflect your personality.

neighborhood matters, especially where these are a source of friction.

- Sparkling white or iridescent jewelry: diamond, white zircon, opal, and rock crystal are most popular. Wear them when dealing with children or working on your own personal creative projects.
- Blue and yellow jewelry: amber, citrine, topaz, tiger's eye, tigeriron, turquoise, and chrysocolla are excellent choices. Wear these crystals when studying, giving presentations, and teaching others.
- Red jewelry: ruby, carnelian, and red amber are most common; red tiger's eye is more unusual, but a good alternative. Wear them when hosting events (parties, dinners, and so on) or in situations that you know, or suspect, may be confrontational.

It is, of course, perfectly acceptable to mix and match crystals as you wish, as long as you don't overload yourself. Small and tasteful is preferable to bold and brash—unless, of course, bold and brash is your personal style. If you overdo your jewelry, you run the risk of not being taken seriously.

First impressions are important, and it's often surprising how accurate they are. Remember, though, that it's what is inside that counts, rather than the external wrapping, so it's wise not to try to be someone other than yourself. You want people to remember you for your personality and talents, rather than for what you're wearing. That said, crystals are beautiful, and wearing them should make you feel beautiful as well. So enjoy them, use them to help further your dreams and ideals, and start making the world a better place.

A traditional jade dragon pendant for long life, health, protection, and good fortune—this is a talisman that anyone can wear.

INDEX

ACKNOWLEDGMENTS

Picture credits

Banana Stock 110, 112–113. **Corbis UK Ltd** 119; / C/B Productions 125. **Getty Images** 138; /Romilly Lockyer 56; /Julie Toy 42. **Image Source** 19, 40, 81. **Octopus Publishing Group Limited** 91; /Frazer Cunningham 2 left, 2 right, 5 left, 5 right, 6, 17, 21, 27, 31, 35, 37, 39, 41, 45, 47, 48, 51, 53, 57, 63, 65, 69, 71, 73, 75, 78, 82, 85, 87, 92–93, 94, 99 right, 101, 108, 115, 120, 122, 131 top left, 133, 134–135, 137, 141; /Walter Gardiner 140; /Sebastian Hedgecoe 20, 106; /Mike Hemsley 11 bottom left, 15 top left, 15 bottom left, 29 top right, 74 left, 88 bottom center, 89 bottom center, 99 top left, 102 bottom right, 105 bottom center, 113 bottom left, 118 left, 131 bottom right, 132 bottom left; /Neil Hepworth 61; /Alistair Hughes 38; /Andy Komorowski 9 bottom left, 12 bottom right, 18 bottom left, 18 bottom center right, 29 bottom center right, 34 bottom right, 43 top right, 43 bottom right, 62, 71 center left, 81 bottom right, 95, 102 bottom center, 104 bottom left, 104 bottom center, 105 center right, 123 bottom left, 124 bottom right, 131 bottom left, 136 bottom left, 136 bottom center, 139; /Mike Prior 15 top right, 18 bottom right, 23, 24, 60 bottom right, 60 bottom center, 64 center right, 88 bottom left, 96 left, 111 center right, 130 right, 132 bottom right; /Tom Mannion 33; /William Reavell 25; /Guy Ryecart 1, 8 bottom left, 8 bottom right, 9 top left, 9 bottom right, 10 bottom right, 10 bottom left, 10 bottom center, 11 bottom center, 11 bottom right, 12 top right, 13 top left, 13 bottom right, 13 bottom left, 15 bottom right, 15 bottom center left, 15 bottom center right, 15 top center right, 15 top center left, 18 bottom center left, 26, 28 bottom right, 28 bottom left, 28 bottom center, 29 bottom right, 29 top center right, 32 bottom right, 32 bottom left, 32 bottom center, 34 top right, 34 bottom center right, 34 top center right, 36 bottom right, 36 bottom left, 36 bottom center, 43 center right, 46 top right, 46 center right, 46 bottom right, 49 top left, 49 bottom right, 49 bottom center right, 49 top center right, 50 bottom right, 50 bottom left, 50 bottom center, 52 top right, 52 center right, 52 top center right, 55 center right, 55 bottom right, 60 bottom left, 64 center left, 64 bottom right, 64 bottom left, 67 bottom right, 67 bottom left, 67 bottom center, 67 bottom center left, 67 bottom center right, 68 left, 68 right, 71 top left, 71 bottom left, 74 right, 77 top right, 77 center right, 77 bottom right, 79, 80 center left, 80 bottom center, 84 center left, 84 center, 84 center right, 84 bottom right, 84 bottom left, 84 bottom center, 88 bottom right, 89 bottom right, 89 bottom left, 90, 93, 96 right, 97 left, 97 right, 99 bottom right, 99 bottom center right, 99 top center right, 102 bottom left, 103 top left, 103 top right, 103 bottom right, 103 bottom left, 103 bottom center, 104 bottom right, 105 top right, 105 bottom left, 105 bottom right, 107 center left, 107 center, 107 center right, 107 bottom center, 116 bottom right, 116 bottom center left, 116 bottom center right, 117 bottom right, 117 bottom left, 117 bottom center, 118 right, 120 center left, 120 center right, 120 bottom center, 123 top left, 123 bottom center left, 123 top center left, 127 right, 127 bottom left, 127 bottom center, 130 left, 132 bottom center, 136 bottom right; /Russell Sadur 54–55, 89; /David Sarton/Orchard Pottery, RHS Chelsea Flower Show 2002 97 top left; /Unit Photographic 22, 59, 66; /Mark Winwood 126. **Red Cover**/James Hudson 128.

Executive Editor Brenda Rosen
Project Editor Leanne Bryan
Executive Art Editor Sally Bond
Designer Simon Wilder
Photographer Frazer Cunningham
Picture Librarian Jennifer Veall
Production Controller Simone Nauerth

About the authors

For further information about the writing partnership of Ken and Joules Taylor, visit their website www.wavewrights.com